OLD TESTAMENT MESSAGE

A Biblical-Theological Commentary

Carroll Stuhlmueller, C.P. and Martin McNamara, M.S.C.

EDITORS

Old Testament Message, Volume 14

LAMENTATIONS, HAGGAI, ZECHARIAH, MALACHI, OBADIAH, JOEL, SECOND ZECHARIAH, BARUCH

Jerome Kodell, O.S.B.

Michael Glazier, Inc.
Wilmington, Delaware

First published in 1982 by:
MICHAEL GLAZIER, INC.
1723 Delaware Avenue
Wilmington, Delaware 19806

Distributed outside U.S., Canada & the Philippines by:
GILL & MACMILLAN, LTD.
Goldenbridge, Inchicore
Dublin 8 Ireland

Library of Congress Catalog Card Number: 81-80824
International Standard Book Number
  Old Testament Message series: 0-89453-235-9
  LAMENTATIONS, HAGGAI, ZECHARIAH, SECOND ZECHARIAH,
  MALACHI, OBADIAH, JOEL, BARUCH
  0-89453-248-0 (Michael Glazier, Inc.)
  7171-1178-4 (Gill and Macmillan, Ltd.)

Cartography by Lucille Dragovan
Cover design by Lillian Brulc
Typography by Robert Zerbe/Graphics

Printed in the United States of America

TABLE OF CONTENTS

Editors' Preface   vii

Introduction   xi

Lamentations   1

Haggai   45

Zechariah   61

Malachi   91

Historical Supplement: Nehemiah and Ezra   111

Obadiah   119

Joel   131

Second Zechariah   155

Baruch   187

For My Father And My Mother

Editors' Preface

Old Testament Message brings into our life and religion today the ancient word of God to Israel. This word, according to the book of the prophet Isaiah, had soaked the earth like "rain and snow coming gently down from heaven" and had returned to God fruitfully in all forms of human life (Isa 55:10). The authors of this series remain true to this ancient Israelite heritage and draw us into the home, the temple and the marketplace of God's chosen people. Although they rely upon the tools of modern scholarship to uncover the distant places and culture of the biblical world, yet they also refocus these insights in a language clear and understandable for any interested reader today. They enable us, even if this be our first acquaintance with the Old Testament, to become sister and brother, or at least good neighbor, to our religious ancestors. In this way we begin to hear God's word ever more forcefully in our own times and across our world, within our prayer and worship, in our secular needs and perplexing problems.

Because life is complex and our world includes, at times in a single large city, vastly different styles of living, we have much to learn from the Israelite Scriptures. The Old Testament spans forty-six biblical books and almost nineteen hundred years of life. It extends through desert, agricultural and urban ways of human existence. The literary style embraces a world of literature and human emotions. Its history began with Moses and the birth-pangs of a new people, it came of age politically and economically under David and Solomon, it reeled under the fiery threats of prophets like Amos and Jeremiah. The people despaired and yet were re-created with new hope during the Babylonian exile. Later reconstruction in the homeland and then the trauma of apocalyptic movements prepared for the revelation of "the mystery hidden for ages in God who created all things" (Eph 3:9).

While the Old Testament telescopes twelve to nineteen hundred years of human existence within the small country of Israel, any single moment of time today witnesses to the reenactment of this entire history across the wide expanse of planet earth. Each verse of the Old Testament is being relived somewhere in our world today. We need, therefore, the *entire* Old Testament and all twenty-three volumes of this new set, in order to be totally a "Bible person" within today's widely diverse society.

The subtitle of this series—"A Biblical-Theological Commentary"—clarifies what these twenty-three volumes intend to do.

Their *purpose* is theological: to feel the pulse of God's word for its *religious* impact and direction.

Their *method* is biblical: to establish the scriptural word firmly within the life and culture of ancient Israel.

Their *style* is commentary: not to explain verse by verse but to follow a presentation of the message that is easily understandable to any serious reader, even if this person is untrained in ancient history and biblical languages.

Old Testament Message—like its predecessor, *New Testament Message*—is aimed at the entire English-speaking world and so is a collaborative effort of an international team. The twenty-one contributors are women and men drawn from North America, Ireland, Britain and Australia. They are scholars who have published in scientific journals, but they have been chosen equally as well for their proven ability to communicate on a popular level. This twenty-three book set comes from Roman Catholic writers, yet, like the Bible itself, it reaches beyond interpretations restricted to an individual church and so enables men and women rooted in biblical faith to unite and so to appreciate their own traditions more fully and more adequately.

Most of all, through the word of God, we seek the blessedness and joy of those

who walk in the law of the Lord!...

who seek God with their whole heart (Ps. 119:1-2).

Carroll Stuhlmueller, C.P.   Martin McNamara, M.S.C.

THE BIBLICAL BOOKS IN HISTORY

626 Call of Jeremiah
612 Babylonians overthrow Assyrian royal city, Nineveh
609 Death of King Josiah of Judah
605 Babylonians defeat Egyptians at Carchemish
597 Judah's leaders deported to Babylon
587 Destruction of Jerusalem; general deportation
LAMENTATIONS
539 Cyrus the Great defeats Babylon
538 End of Exile
Sheshbazzar leads first return to Jerusalem
520 **HAGGAI**
520-518 **ZECHARIAH (Zech 1 - 8)**
515 New Temple completed
460 **MALACHI**
445-395 Reformation of Nehemiah and Ezra
400-380 **OBADIAH**
JOEL
333 Alexander the Great defeats Persia
325 **SECOND ZECHARIAH (Zech 9 - 14)**
312 Judea under the rule of the Ptolomies (Egyptian)
200 Judea under the rule of the Seleucids (Syrian)
180 **BARUCH**
175 Seleucid Antiochus IV Epiphanes begins oppression
167-164 Maccabean War of Liberation

NATIONS AND THEIR RULERS

Judah		*Babylon*	
640-609	Josiah	625-605	Nabopolasser
609	Jehoahaz	604-562	Nebuchadnezzar
609-598	Jehoiakim	561-560	Awil-Marduk
598-597	Jehoiachin	559-556	Nergal-shar-usur
597-587	Zedekiah	556	Labashi-Marduk
587	Fall of Judah	555-539	Nabonidus
		539	Fall of Babylon

Persia

559-529	Cyrus the Great
528-522	Cambyses II
521-486	Darius I
486-465	Xerxes I
465-425	Artaxerxes I Longimanus
424-404	Darius II Nothos
404-359	Artaxerxes II Mnemon
359-338	Artaxerxes III Ochus
338-336	Arses
336-333	Darius III Condomannus
333	Fall of Persia

Greece

336-323	Alexander the Great
After 323	Kingdom divided among Ptolemies and Seleucids

INTRODUCTION

WHEN FIRST THEY TOLD YOU you didn't believe it. You had been away from home a long time, perhaps as a soldier stationed far away, or unable to return home because of some other obligation or because of sickness. The news came that your family home had been devastated by fire or storm, and all the familiar landmarks had been eradicated. The great oak tree was down; old Shep had been killed. A letter from your sister mentioned that a change had come over your parents; something had gone out of them.

You were shocked and saddened. Tears came as you remembered the many associations of childhood and growing up and reunions. But as days passed the pain softened. Optimism began to return. This is tragic, but it's not final. We'll come out of this. We'll rebuild or start something new. Finally as you neared home, you were fearful and anxious about the ruin you would see and about the condition of your family, but anxiety was giving way to hope. It can't be as bad as they said. And then, as you made the turn that gave you your first glimpse of the old home place, your heart went to your throat and tears glistened in your eyes again. It was even worse than you'd imagined. You were seized with a great sense of loss and pain.

This is the way it was for the Hebrews who looked upon the devastation that had been Jerusalem, their holy city, after it was ravaged by the Babylonians. The pain was so

great it could scarcely be suffered. Surely this was the end
of hope. The God of Israel had abandoned his people. The
time had come for weeping and despair. But it was not the
end of hope. Israel's remnant reached deep into the ancient
faith for resources to build hope again out of the ashes of
Jerusalem. Once more, hope found expression in Hebrew
poetry and prophecy. The new generation recorded its
experience of agony and recovery, defeat and regeneration,
as the people of God struggled out of the Exile into a new
life in Israel.

Years ago Pope Pius XII urged us in reading the ancient
texts of Scripture to "go back wholly in spirit to those
remote centuries of the East" (*Divino Afflante Spiritu*, 35),
to experience vicariously the time, the situation, the emotions of the people. The biblical books gathered in this
volume take us into the heart of Israel's most bitter experience as a nation, the destruction of her temple and city
and the exile of her people in Babylon, and lead us through
the poignant memories of return and restoration. They
cover a period of five hundred years, from the deportation
of 587 B.C. (Lamentations) to the first century B.C.
(Baruch). Other biblical writings were produced during
this time (for example, 1-2 Chronicles, Ezra, Nehemiah,
Ruth, Jonah) which contribute in their own way to com-
pleting the picture of exilic and post-exilic Israel. But the
present collection makes a coherent reflection on the ups
and downs of the period, and is especially valuable in
describing (and exhibiting) the deep emotions of the people
as they reacted to the events.

The Exile

Contrary to the urgings of Jeremiah, King Jehoiakim
of Judah (609-598 B.C.) revolted against Israel's Babylonian
overlords when Babylon was momentarily weakened by
war with Egypt (601). He had underestimated the resiliency
of this world power, and retaliation against Jerusalem was
swift and decisive. The city surrendered to King Nebuchadnezzar in mid-March, 597, three months after Jehoiakim

had died (perhaps murdered) and been succeeded by his son, Jehoiachin. The new king was taken into exile in Babylon along with the leading citizens: ". . . all the princes, and all the mighty men of valor, ten thousand captives, and all the craftsmen and the smiths" (2 Kgs 24:14). The Babylonians placed Zedekiah, brother of Jehoiakim, on the throne of Judah. He was weak and vacillating, one minute listening to Jeremiah, the next to the pro-Egyptian party. He finally gave in to the latter, following exactly the course set by his ill-fated brother. Once again, the vengeance of Babylon was quick, but this time the invaders saw to it that there would be no more uprisings. They destroyed the Temple, broke down the walls of the city and burned it, and took the balance of the population into exile (2 Kgs 25:8-12).

It seemed like the end of the world. The impossible had happened. Yahweh, the God of Israel, had proved powerless in the moment of crisis. He had been defeated by the gods of foreign nations. The pillars of the faith were shattered: God had deserted the land; the holy city and the Temple had passed into the hands of invaders, and the chosen people were scattered to foreign lands. Some of the exiles lost faith altogether. But there were others whose faith held firm. They remained convinced of the lordship of Yahweh and his care and concern for his people, interpreting the disaster as just punishment for sin.

The long years of exile tested and purified the faith of these people. They brought their excruciating sense of loss into their prayer:

"O God, the heathens have come into thy inheritance;
they have defiled thy holy temple;
they have laid Jerusalem in ruins . . . .
Help us, O God of our salvation,
for the glory of thy name;
deliver us, and forgive our sins,
for thy name's sake!" (Ps 79:1,9)

The religious leaders gathered the ancient traditions, both spoken and written, into narratives and poetic collections, awaiting the day of restoration which exiled prophets (Ezekiel, Second Isaiah) assured them would come.

Meanwhile, there were still some Jews left in the shell of Jerusalem. Some of these had probably avoided the deportation. Others had returned from self-imposed exile to ponder the desolation of the city. This is the setting for the first book to be treated in our commentary, Lamentations. It was produced soon after the deportation of 587 by a gifted Hebrew believer who was able to express profound pain and sadness in memorable poetry. This, probably more than any detailed chronicle could, takes us "back in spirit" to the Hebrew experience of the loss of the Temple and the holy city.

The Return

Thirty-five years after the destruction and deportation, the exiles' hopes were aroused by news that Babylon was beginning to be threatened by a new major power, the Persians under King Cyrus (Isa 45:1). Cyrus gradually consolidated his forces until in 539 he defeated the Babylonian army at the Tigris River and took the kingship away from Nabonidus. One year later he issued a decree permitting the Hebrew exiles to return to their homeland (Ezra 1:2-4). This was in line with his policy of religious tolerance for subjugated nations. He even gave financial support to the project and returned sacred vessels of the temple that had been plundered by Nebuchadnezzar.

The first exiles to return were mostly natives of Judah and Benjamin (roughly the Jerusalem area). They were led by Sheshbazzar, a "prince of Judah" (Ezra 1:8) with a Babylonian name who was appointed governor. Under his leadership the foundations of the new Temple were laid (Ezra 5:14-16). His name disappears from the records at this point and his place is taken by another exiled

Hebrew, Zerubbabel, who along with the priest Joshua became the focus of new hope in the Jerusalem community. These leaders followed through energetically with the work of Temple reconstruction (Ezra 3:8-9), only to meet stiff opposition from local residents who had moved into the abandoned land during the Exile, and from their Samaritan neighbors to the north (Ezra 4). These enemies were able to bring pressure from Persia to wilt the enthusiasm of the returnees, causing them to abandon their project for a later time. Instead of raising a new Temple, they devoted their time to building up their own houses and scratching out an existence in the ruined land.

When by 520 B.C. the Temple still lay in ruins, two prophets, Haggai and Zechariah, raised their voices to decry the laxity and lethargy of a people who had forgotten their exilic hopes and their promises to build the Lord a new house. The ministry of these two prophets roused the people to action, so that by 515 a new Temple stood where the old one had been. But there was disappointment mixed with the joy of achievement. The new Temple could not compare with the glorious Temple of Solomon. Oldtimers who remembered the first Temple from childhood wept when they saw what had taken its place. The new Temple was in its own way a symbol for the returnees of their disillusionment during the twenty years since the edict of Cyrus. They had dreamed of a glorious march into Jerusalem by the thousands, but their numbers were relatively small. Many of their compatriots had let the hope of return die as they made peace with the land of exile. They had envisioned a renewal of the Davidic empire, and they were crowded into a small circle in Judah. There had been the unforeseen hostility of the people who had home-steaded the land during their absence. And now, instead of the reconstruction of a Temple on Solomonic lines, they had to be satisfied with a much smaller and less glorious building. The triumph of surviving the Exile was bittersweet.

A Hundred Years Later

Even though the new Temple was not as imposing as some would have liked, it did serve to focus the religious traditions and hopes of Israel once again. Zerubbabel, like Sheshbazzar, mysteriously disappeared from view and no successor was appointed as governor. The result of this was that the leadership of the new community was taken over by Joshua and his priestly successors. The Temple became the center of political as well as religious authority.

Toward the middle of the fifth century a voice was raised against abuses precisely in the priesthood and at the Temple. Malachi lashed out against the priests for misleading the people and "corrupting the covenant" (Mal 2:8), for allowing abuses in the liturgy, intermarriage with foreigners, and the spread of social injustice. As usual, stability had led to the abuses of complacency. News of this state of affairs reached Babylon, where many Jews still remained. The cupbearer of the Persian ruler, Artaxerxes, was Nehemiah, a descendant of exiles. He heard about the abuses, but also about the continued hostility of neighboring provinces, and most shattering for him, that the ancient city wall had still not been rebuilt (Neh 1:1-4).

Nehemiah prevailed on the king to send him back to Jerusalem to rebuild the wall. He fulfilled this mission with great courage and endurance and served as governor in Jerusalem for twelve years (445-433 B.C.). Some time later a priest and scribe, Ezra, received a commission from the Persian authorities to institute a complete religious reform and call the people back to the Mosaic Law. His work was just as successful as Nehemiah's. He read the ancient Law to the people, presided over the ratification of the covenant, and instituted strict marriage reforms. Jerusalem entered a new era of stability and fervor.

Two documents in our commentary are datable to the immediate aftermath of the work of Nehemiah and Ezra (about 400 B.C.): Obadiah and Joel. Obadiah reflected on the fall of Edom, an ancient enemy of Israel, during this time, seeing its decline as a sign of the downfall of all Israel's enemies and the establishment of Yahweh's kingship. The prophecy of Joel was more closely related to the effect of the recent reforms. His community had rallied around the Temple and the Law. They were stunned by the onslaught of a devastating locust invasion which seemed sure to bring much sickness, and Joel saw in this plague a sign of the terrors of judgment and punishment on the "day of the Lord." He called the community to prayer; the plague ceased. Joel prophesied a glorious salvation for Israel and the destruction of her enemies. But the religious reform of Ezra had provoked the beginning of a narrow nationalism and siege mentality that other writers would have to dismantle.

Later Times

There is another jump of a hundred years to the next book in our series. It is a writing that does not ostensibly stand alone, because it has been joined to an earlier work, the Book of Zechariah. Chapters Nine through Fourteen of Zechariah do not belong to the sixth-century prophet but come from an anonymous author (or authors) writing in the latter third of the fourth century B.C. This section of the book is often referred to as Second Zechariah; the process by which it was connected to the earlier book will be discussed in the commentary.

The meteoric rise of Alexander the Great and the consequent overthrow of the ruling Persian dynasty aroused hopes that the decisive establishment of God's reign was close at hand. This sort of reaction had happened before, for example when Cyrus defeated the Babylonians (Isaiah 40-55) and when Darius I's hold on the Persian Kingdom seemed about to slip (Haggai, Zechariah 1-8). Messianic expectancy made some Hebrews acutely sensitive to the signs of God's interventions in history. Second Zechariah foresaw a terrible struggle which would purify God's people for the kingdom of God. Jerusalem would emerge from the final battle as the center of the world. All the

survivors of the foreign nations would make pilgrimage
to the holy city to celebrate the most popular Jewish
festival, the Feast of Booths (Zech 14:16-19).

The final book in our series, Baruch, takes us to within
one hundred years of the birth of Jesus. Two centuries
and a half have passed since the triumphs of Alexander.
The decisive victory of Yahweh has not yet come after all.
The Jews seem to the writer of this book to have become complacent and relaxed, forgetful of the people
and events of the past that made it possible for them to
live in the holy land of their fathers, with a Temple and
priesthood in place. Echoes of exilic times are very remote.

To stir his contemporaries out of their lethargy, the
author of Baruch recreates the situation of a group of
exiles in faraway Babylon shortly after the deportation
of 587. He compiles earlier writings and liturgical prayers
along with his own under the name of Baruch, the secretary of Jeremiah, calling for a return to the sources of
Hebrew faith and seeking to instill a sense of solidarity
with the suffering exiles of ancient times.

Today's Reader

The books selected for this volume in the Old Testament
Message series are among the least familiar to Christian
readers. Snatches of individual books are familiar from
their use in the New Testament or in the liturgy: Lamentations for Good Friday Reproaches, Malachi for the Gospel
descriptions of John the Baptist, Joel for Peter's Pentecost
sermon in Acts, Second Zechariah for images and terminology used in the Passion accounts. But by and large
these short biblical books are seldom read or studied.
They do not have the appeal of the creation stories, the
historical narratives, the oracles of the great prophets, the
psalms, or the maxims of the wisdom literature.

And yet, perhaps they could have a special appeal to
the Christian (or the Jew) of today. These books were
produced after a great watershed in Old Testament history,
the destruction of Jerusalem and the deportation of God's

people into exile. The writers instinctively recoil from the thought of what has happened; they speak in horror and disbelief; they tell of the reluctance of the returned exiles to accept a new situation and live within it creatively and constructively. There is a spirit of looking back to the good old days that bespeaks a people past its prime. Only grudgingly and gradually does Israel look to the future; and not to the near future, in which a new existence will have to be realistically carved out of defeats and disappointments, but to a distant and idealized future to be unveiled by the decisive judgment of God.

Today's religious person stands on the far side of a similar watershed. The clear colors of a much simpler religious past are still fresh in our memories. We can hardly believe the changes in religious consciousness, the shift in moral awareness, the fragmenting of a system of agreed norms and ideals. We experience the temptation to throw up our hands or to hide our heads in hopelessness because we can never recover what has been lost. It is hard to accept the challenge to build creatively in the current situation without falling into a search for the irretrievable good old things of the past.

For many Catholics this malaise clusters vaguely around Vatican Council II, not the actual Council with the documents and reforms it produced, but a larger-than-life event which serves as a symbol around which to focus disappointments. Every period of history looks better once we are through it and looking back. Egypt was a place of unbearable enslavement for the Israelites until they escaped into the desert; then they looked back fondly and idealized their bondage. Later on the great prophets would glamorize the desert wandering while scoring the evils of the monarchy. The exiles glamorized the monarchy. Today's Catholic idealizes the Church of the Thirties, Forties and Fifties, forgetting the complaints that swirled and rumbled in those days.

This is not to say that there is never any solid basis for disappointment. The renewal of Vatican II has been less glorious than its heralds foresaw, just as the return to

Jerusalem and the restoration of the nation was an immense disappointment. The new Temple, which paled by (imagined) comparison with the Temple of Solomon, was surely the focus for a whole cluster of restoration woes. Valuable things were lost in the shuffle after Vatican II; they must, if possible, be recovered. But that is just the point. The search for old valuables must be a realistic one, not a probing for sacred vessels in a ruined Temple, wasting renewal energy while overlooking the positive gains of the new situation. The Church of Vatican II is emerging; there is still a long way to go. But the pre-Vatican II Church will never come again. Somehow, in God's plan, it is gone forever, like the Jerusalem of the monarchy. Faith says that, if God is the Lord of history, something better can be built. But the task must be carried on within a courageous and faith-filled thrust into the present age with its present circumstances. It is foolish and hopeless to wait for the past to return.

The biblical books studied in this volume were born of shattered dreams. In them we find the various stages of response to tragedy: disbelief and hopelessness, acceptance, grasping recklessly at signs of hope, momentary enthusiasm and momentary despair, tentative planning for the future and a new age. Jews and Christians look to biblical history for people and events to interpret and pattern their own lives: a journey of faith like Abraham's, a liberation from slavery like Moses', a repentance like David's, a ministry of the word like Jeremiah's.

These books produced in the Exile and afterwards show a people rising out of the ashes, slowly and haphazardly. In them we read of defeat and catch tones of bitterness and hatefulness as well as of patience and hope. But these books are undergirded by faith. Otherwise they would never have been written or preserved, and we would not have them to read. They are a response of faith to a flawed situation. They disappoint us and then surprise us. They can help us respond to and understand our own dilemmas as we grow out of the past and into the future.

Lamentations

LAMENTATIONS

Background
IN THE INTRODUCTION, the destruction of Jerusalem
and the sacred temple was compared to the loss of an
ancestral home. If it had been your family home, and its
loss had meant bitter agony for you and your family, how
would you have described the tragedy to those who heard
about it later? How long would it have taken you to describe
the house, its nooks and corners, the surroundings, and
the beauty of the place as a living unity? A complete picture
would have included a certain amount of family history
and many disconnected memories; it would have involved
personalities and relationships and have been full of
impressions from early childhood to adulthood.

The writer who produced Lamentations was faced with
such an apparently impossible task. The whole history of
the people and all the memories of the city and its inhabitants were pushing and shoving to get into the story. How
deliver to others the experience of the loss of Jerusalem?
The answer was simple and brilliant: to go directly to the
heart of the still-throbbing pain and try to capture the
feeling and record it in poetic imagery. A feeling cannot
remain alive on paper; feeling lives only in human hearts.
But authentic poetry can bring a unique human feeling to
life in other hearts, igniting it again like new fire struck
from flint. Descriptions of history and relationships and

3

memories can go on endlessly, building up the mind's understanding of the tragedy, without ever reaching the experience of a heart. But a poetic sharing of the feeling can go immediately to the heart.

This is what happens in the Book of Lamentations. It shimmers with tragedy. The feeling of loss rolls over the reader in wave after wave. There is no systematic progression of thought in Lamentations; if there is any progression, it is one of feeling, a progression of moods. The sensation of loss and pain is as severe at the beginning as it will be at the end, but different aspects of the tragedy come in for mention as the poetry throbs along. It is as if we were reading the mind of the sufferer, following his stream of consciousness. There are sudden flashes of repetition, seemingly with no relation to the course of thought. But this is the way it is in inconsolable loss, for a person who has lost an arm or leg, for a wife whose husband has died, for a father whose son has been killed in war: the mind tries to think of other things, to stay out of the dangerous channels; but the loss and its consequences are lurking just beyond consciousness and the images are continually reappearing and flooding the memory.

Authorship

We do not know who wrote Lamentations. All the indications point to its composition in Jerusalem soon after its fall to the Babylonians and the final deportation of citizens in 587 B.C. This episode and the earlier deportation of certain leaders (597 B.C.) are described in 2 Kings 24-25 and Jeremiah 39 and 52. It is possible that there was more than one writer and that the poems were written at different times. In our discussion we will speak of a single writer active shortly after the destruction and deportation of 587.

The book became entitled "The Lamentations of Jeremiah" when it was translated into Greek around 200 B.C. But in the Hebrew Bible, Lamentations is found in the section called Writings, rather than with Jeremiah in the

Prophets section. It is part of a unique group of five books called *Megilloth*, or the "Scrolls," designated for liturgical use on five important Jewish feasts. The books stand in the order of the calendar in the Hebrew Bible: Song of Songs for Passover (spring), Ruth for Pentecost (early summer), Lamentations for the Ninth of Ab (midsummer), Ecclesiastes for Tabernacles (fall), and Esther for Purim (late winter). The Ninth of Ab (or *Tishoh B'Ov*) commemorates the fall of Jerusalem to the Romans and the destruction of the Herodian Temple in 70 A.D. The plaintive poems re-create for Jewish worshipers the sentiments of pain and loss associated with this tragedy and the earlier invasion of the Babylonians.

The Greek translators moved the book from its original position in the Hebrew canon to stand after the prophecy of Jeremiah. The Latin Vulgate followed this tradition and our English translations were influenced by this Greek-Latin usage. The reasons for associating Lamentations with Jeremiah are obvious. He had foretold the destruction of the city and described the suffering to come as punishment for the sins of the people in the same terms as Lamentations; he was not taken into Babylon himself, but remained in the wasted city for at least a short time before being forcibly evacuated to Egypt. The author of Chronicles describes Jeremiah as the author of a lament for King Josiah (2 Chr 35:25), who had been killed in battle at Megiddo twenty years earlier. Perhaps the notion of "lament" also influenced the connection of Jeremiah with this later book.

But the evidence for Jeremiah's authorship of Lamentations is hardly more than circumstantial. There are strong internal reasons against it. He would not have associated himself with those hoping for help from Egypt (Lam 4:17; compare Jer 37:3-10). It is not likely that he would have described the ruler in the glowing terms of Lamentations (4:20). Besides, scholars point out significant differences in vocabulary and poetic style. Ultimately, of course, the personal identity of the author is of little importance; he is writing as one of the people trying to describe their experience of the loss of Jerusalem through a portrayal of his own feeling.

Structure

Our modern Bibles are divided into chapters and verses, but this practice is a relatively recent development in the history of the Bible. Though ancient manuscripts had marginal signs to indicate the beginning of new sections, the systematic division of the biblical books into chapters was first done by Stephen Langton in 1226, while the text was not separated into verses until the sixteenth century. This division has been very helpful to readers and was executed with generally good judgment, but since the editors weren't able to consult the authors they occasionally divided the text in ways that could have puzzled the author.

But we have clear indications from the author of Lamentations that the chapter divisions of our modern Bibles are where they should be. Each chapter contains a section intended by the author to stand by itself. He showed this (in Hebrew) by an alphabetic acrostic: each chapter has twenty-two verses, the number of letters in the Hebrew alphabet (though Chapter Three is printed as sixty-six verses because it has sixty-six lines). Each verse of Chapters One through Four begins with a different letter of the alphabet in order. When the chapter reaches *tau*, the final letter, the poem is complete. Chapter Five has twenty-two verses but not in alphabetical order. Ronald Knox's English translation imitates this alphabetic arrangement of the Hebrew.

What is the purpose of this poetic technique? For one thing, it gives a sense of the unity of the poems, which might not be so clear in Lamentations, where the intention is the creation of mood rather than the progression of thoughts or images. It might also be a way of indicating the depth, thoroughness, or universality of the tragic feeling being portrayed: from A to Z.

Reading the Book

The history of the use of Lamentations in the Jewish and Christian communities is quite instructive for its use by the individual believer. The book and the emotions it carries will never disappear from the Jewish and Christian consciousness because it has been given an important place in Jewish and Christian liturgy. As mentioned earlier, the book is read on the Ninth of Ab in the synagogue, and its imagery and cadences form the core of the Reproaches of the Christian Good Friday liturgy. In both instances the emotion captured in the Jerusalem of the Exile has been applied to later tragedies of salvation history: for the Jew, the fall of Jerusalem to the Romans and the destruction of the Herodian Temple; for the Christian, the suffering and death of Jesus.

This use of an authentic spiritual experience as the basis for prayer in later times and circumstances is also the rationale for many of the psalms. A true experience of God in triumph or in trial is captured poetically in the psalms and remains available to express the God-experience of later believers. Synagogue and Church use the psalms and Lamentations for community prayer; and individuals use them for personal prayer. Lamentations may be read privately in the name of the Church or a local community, expressing the sense of loss that has gripped a group of people; it may be the basis of a prayer for a suffering friend; it may express one's own sense of pain and loss through a bitter trial. Like the psalms, Lamentations provides us with inspired words that speak for us when we cannot find adequate words of our own.

FIRST LAMENTATION

THE FIRST LAMENTATION falls equally into two parts. Verses 1-11 are the description of Jerusalem by a visitor who had known her former splendor and is now appalled by the destruction she has suffered. In verses 12-24 the city herself speaks, taking us into her own painful misery.

YESTERDAY'S PRINCESS
1:1-3

1 How lonely sits the city that was full of people!
How like a widow has she become,
   she that was great among the nations!
She that was a princess among the cities
   has become a vassal.

²She weeps bitterly in the night,
   tears on her cheeks;
among all her lovers
   she has none to comfort her;
all her friends have dealt treacherously with her,
   they have become her enemies.

³Judah has gone into exile because of affliction
   and hard servitude;
she dwells now among the nations,
   but finds no resting place;
her pursuers have all overtaken her
   in the midst of her distress.

First to strike the visitor's eye is the contrast of present emptiness to the earlier hustle and bustle of a thriving city. "How lonely sits the city that was full of people!" The word "how" used this way to note a striking change of fortune, from riches to rags, from happiness to sorrow, is a typical way to start a funeral song. The poems in Chapters Two and Four begin the same way. It is also used in taunt songs: "How you have vanished from the seas, O city renowned (Tyre)!" (Ezek 26:17); "How the oppressor has ceased, the insolent fury ceased (Babylon)!" (Isa 14:4). This first word of the Hebrew text, "How" (*'ekāh*), serves as the Hebrew title of the book.

It is typical for the prophets and psalms to picture Jerusalem as a woman, the "daughter of Zion" (Pss 9:15; 73:28), "virgin daughter Zion" (Isa 37:22). Jeremiah has a special fondness for the term "daughter of my people" (Jer 4:11; 6:14,26; 8:19-22) which Lamentations uses as a term of endearment several times (e.g. 1:6; 2:1,13) with special poignancy. But only once is Jerusalem described as a widow, in the very first verse. The widow in Israel, like the orphan, is a sad and tragic figure. The widow and orphan were defenseless. Concern for their welfare is regularly expressed in Hebrew literature (Exod 22:22; Deut 10:18; Ps 146:9; Job 29:13); it was a terrible curse to wish one an orphan or widow (Ps 109:9). Jerusalem has been a great one among the nations, one in command and control; now she is a widow, at the mercy of all. She was a princess, now she must be a handmaid. Though it is not so stated, perhaps Zion as daughter is here to be considered an orphan. Jerusalem's new status as widow is emphasized by the repetition of the plaint "There is none to comfort her" in verses 2, 9, 16, 17 and 21.

Israel had made alliances with many of her neighbors over the years. Often this was done against the advice of her prophets (Isa 7; 28). Now that Jerusalem was in trouble none of these allies came forth to support her. They have even taken advantage of her fall to enrich themselves. Judah has gone into exile "*from* affliction and hard servitude" is a better translation than "because of" (v.3). Judah's recent history had seen much suffering, and exile was simply another way, a new way for her, of experiencing pain.

SUFFERING FOR TRANSGRESSIONS
1:4-11

4The roads to Zion mourn,
for none come to the appointed feasts;
all her gates are desolate,
her priests groan;
her maidens have been dragged away,
and she herself suffers bitterly.

5Her foes have become the head,
her enemies prosper,
because the LORD has made her suffer for the multitude
of her transgressions;
her children have gone away,
captives before the foe.

6From the daughter of Zion has departed
all her majesty.
Her princes have become like harts
that find no pasture;
they fled without strength
before the pursuer.
7Jerusalem remembers in the days of her affliction and
bitterness
all the precious things
that were hers from days of old.
When her people fell into the hand of the foe,
and there was none to help her,
the foe gloated over her
mocking at her downfall.

8Jerusalem sinned grievously,
therefore she became filthy;

all who honored her despise her,
  for they have seen her nakedness;
yea, she herself groans,
  and turns her face away.

⁹Her uncleanness was in her skirts;
  she took no thought of her doom;
therefore her fall is terrible,
  she has no comforter.
"O LORD, behold my affliction,
  for the enemy has triumphed!"

¹⁰The enemy has stretched out his hands
  over all her precious things;
yea, she has seen the nations
  invade her sanctuary,
those whom thou didst forbid
  to enter thy congregation.

¹¹All her people groan
  as they search for bread;
they trade their treasures for food
  to revive their strength.
"Look, O LORD, and behold,
  for I am despised."

Generations of Hebrews had made Jerusalem the focus of
their hopes and the goal of their pilgrimages. Year after
year the people would come up these roads, singing the
songs of Zion, sharing their journey with joyful hearts.
Now the feasts pass unnoticed. No one comes any more.
"The roads to Zion mourn" (v.4)—a particularly expressive
image. The priests cannot perform the roles that were the
highpoint of their service. "Jerusalem remembers" (v.7)
the days of old; at the same time, we know, Jerusalem "is
remembered" by the exiles in Babylon with the same
heartbreak because the Temple with its feasts and thronging
people is no more (Ps 79; 137). "Her uncleanness" (v.9) is

from menstruation, a sign that Jerusalem is ritually impure and a source of impurity for others (Lev 15:19-24).

The narrator does not imply that Jerusalem has been the victim of a capricious or malicious God. "The Lord has made her suffer for the multitude of her transgressions" (v.5); "Jerusalem sinned grievously" (v.8). The fall of Jerusalem is the result of her unfaithfulness. These verses could very well have been written by Jeremiah as a statement of the fulfillment of his warnings (Jer 11:9-11; 25:1-14). The experience of loss permeating Lamentations is not despair. The tragedy suffered by Jerusalem and her people is not a sign that they are cast off by Yahweh or that he is too weak to protect them (a taunt the exiles will hear in Babylon: Ps 42:11). It is rather a sign that he is faithful and just; he promised to punish and purify them. This he has done. He has also promised to take them back; this he will do. Rather than a cry of despair, Lamentations is a prayer. This attitude breaks through in the direct address to the Lord bringing this section to a close. The same kind of direct plea to God will mark the end of each poem.

THE LORD IS IN THE RIGHT
1:12-22

As if to indicate that the view of the narrator-visitor is too cold or uninvolved in its objectivity, the city Jerusalem interrupts: "Look and see if there is any sorrow like my sorrow" (v.12). But there is no whimpering in the lament of the daughter of Zion. Her cry to passersby is a call for compassion, not for defense against an unjust judgment.

> 12"Is it nothing to you, all you who pass by?
>   Look and see
> if there is any sorrow like my sorrow
>   which was brought upon me,
> which the LORD inflicted
>   on the day of his fierce anger.

13"From on high he sent fire;
   into my bones he made it descend;
he spread a net for my feet;
   he turned me back;
he has left me stunned,
   faint all the day long.

14"My transgressions were bound into a yoke;
   by his hand they were fastened together;
they were set upon my neck;
   he caused my strength to fail;
the Lord gave me into the hands
   of those whom I cannot withstand.

15"The Lord flouted all my mighty men
   in the midst of me;
he summoned an assembly against me
   to crush my young men;
the Lord has trodden as in a wine press
   the virgin daughter of Judah.

16"For these things I weep;
   my eyes flow with tears;
for a comforter is far from me,
   one to revive my courage;
my children are desolate,
   for the enemy has prevailed."

17Zion stretches out her hands,
   but there is none to comfort her;
the LORD has commanded against Jacob
   that his neighbors should be his foes;
Jerusalem has become
   a filthy thing among them.

18"The LORD is in the right,
   for I have rebelled against his word;
but hear, all you peoples,
   and behold my suffering;

my maidens and my young men
have gone into captivity.

¹⁹"I called to my lovers
but they deceived me;
my priests and elders
perished in the city,
while they sought food
to revive their strength.
²⁰"Behold, O LORD, for I am in distress,
my soul is in tumult,
my heart is wrung within me,
because I have been very rebellious.
In the street the sword bereaves;
in the house it is like death.

²¹"Hear how I groan;
there is none to comfort me.
All my enemies have heard of my trouble;
they are glad that thou hast done it.
Bring thou the day thou hast announced,
and let them be as I am.

²²"Let all their evil-doing come before thee;
and deal with them
as thou hast dealt with me
because of all my transgressions;
for my groans are many
and my heart is faint."

It is the Lord who has brought this suffering about (v.12), and he is "in the right" (v.18). It is just retribution because of transgressions (v.14), rebellion "against his word" (v.18). This is no sign of his weakness, but rather of his ability to make true his warning. The struggle has not been between Jerusalem and Babylon, but between Jerusalem and Yahweh; the victory of Babylon is only incidental, something allowed because integral to God's plan.

What Jerusalem needs now is not a vindicator against the Lord, but one who will comfort her in her distress, one who will revive her courage (v.16). Out of Zion's cry of pain comes instruction for our own experience of suffering. The lonely city does not cry out aimlessly in her hurt, but is able to identify the hand of the Lord in the crisis, turning her groans toward him but not against him. He is in the right.

The city describes her downfall as a Day of Yahweh (v.12). The prophets, beginning with Amos, had referred to the coming retribution at the end as the Day of the Lord (Amos 5:18-20; Zeph 1:7-10). In Lamentations, uniquely, the day is regarded as already past (see also 2:1, 21, 22). But later in this section Jerusalem calls for the traditional day to come at the end, so that her enemies will receive their just punishment: "Let them be as I am" (v.21). The city's complaint about her suffering amounts really to a proclamation of God's justice. He has dealt fairly with me, and I am fully convinced he will deal fairly with my enemies.

God's work in punishing the daughter of Zion is described in graphic images. He sent fire from on high into her very bones (v.13). There is at least a thematic, if not textual, relationship to the words of Jeremiah in the figure of God's fire. Later she will identify her infidelity as rebelling "against the word" (v.18). Jeremiah described his ministry as a stewardship of the word. When it brought trouble into his life, he was tempted to stop speaking the word:

"If I say, 'I will not mention him,
    or speak any more in his name,'
there is in my heart as it were a burning fire
    shut up in my bones,
and I am weary with holding it in, and I cannot" (Jer 20:9).

The fallen city experienced fire in a material way, but also in this spiritual sense as Jeremiah did, and as we do. In a different image, Jerusalem is compared to a beast of burden or to a slave, on whom the master fastens a yoke made out of sins (v.14). In still another scene, the city is crushed like grapes in the wine press (v.15).

Suddenly the voice of the passerby of the earlier section is heard again (v.17), describing the condition of the city through a reporter's eyes. This interruption of the monologue is a poetic touch to shake the monotony, like the corresponding interruptions of Jerusalem herself in the narrator's part of the chapter (1:9,11). The scattered people is called by a different name, Jacob, a name usually associated with the Northern Kingdom of the divided monarchy (Amos 6:8; Hos 10:11). The Northern Kingdom had fallen to Assyria one hundred fifty years earlier, in 721 B.C.; now the name Jacob is applied to the only Hebrew group left in the land, those of Judah who are now likewise suffering the consequences of their infidelity.

The first poem comes to an end with the summary statement: "My groans are many and my heart is faint." "Groans" is the term used to encompass the outcries of Jerusalem and all her various inhabitants throughout the Chapter. The narrator described the groanings of the priests (v.4) and the people (v.11) and the groanings of the personified city herself (v.8); in her lament, the city asked the passersby to "Hear how I groan" (v.21). With *tau*, the last letter of the alphabet, the final verse wraps into a bundle all the groans of the city and her people.

SECOND LAMENTATION

AS THE SECOND POEM BEGINS, we are back with a third-person narrator. Perhaps a different narrator is intended than in the first chapter, where the poet seemed to be a visitor or passerby (1:12), shocked and saddened by the tragic reversal of the fortunes of the beautiful and powerful city he had known before, but not personally involved in the tragedy. Here the poet seems to be a citizen of Jerusalem and a sharer in her fate. Besides being descriptive, he agonizes over the reason for her punishment (vv.1-17). He will urge her to cry out in prayer (vv.18-19), and finally will call to the Lord in her name and the name of all her inhabitants (vv.20-22).

THE WRATH OF THE LORD
2:1-17

2 How the Lord in his anger
    has set the daughter of Zion under a cloud!
He has cast down from heaven to earth
    the splendor of Israel;
he has not remembered his footstool
    in the day of his anger.

2The Lord has destroyed without mercy
    all the habitations of Jacob;
in his wrath he has broken down
    the strongholds of the daughter of Judah;

he has brought down to the ground in dishonor
the kingdom and its rulers.

³He has cut down in fierce anger
all the might of Israel;
he has withdrawn from them his right hand
in the face of the enemy;
he has burned like a flaming fire in Jacob,
consuming all around.

⁴He has bent his bow like an enemy,
with his right hand set like a foe;
and he has slain all the pride of our eyes
in the tent of the daughter of Zion;
he has poured out his fury like fire.

⁵The Lord has become like an enemy,
he has destroyed Israel;
he has destroyed all its palaces,
laid in ruins its strongholds;
and he has multiplied in the daughter of Judah
mourning and lamentation.

⁶He has broken down his booth like that of a garden,
laid in ruins the place of his appointed feasts;
the LORD has brought to an end in Zion
appointed feast and sabbath,
and in his fierce indignation has spurned
king and priest.

⁷The Lord has scorned his altar,
disowned his sanctuary;
he has delivered into the hand of the enemy
the walls of her palaces;
a clamor was raised in the house of the LORD
as on the day of an appointed feast.

⁸The LORD determined to lay in ruins
the wall of the daughter of Zion;
he marked it off by the line;
he restrained not his hand from destroying;

he caused rampart and wall to lament,
    they languish together.

⁹Her gates have sunk into the ground;
    he has ruined and broken her bars;
her king and princes are among the nations;
    the law is no more,
and her prophets obtain
    no vision from the LORD.

¹⁰The elders of the daughter of Zion
    sit on the ground in silence;
they have cast dust on their heads
    and put on sackcloth;
the maidens of Jerusalem
    have bowed their heads to the ground.

¹¹My eyes are spent with weeping;
    my soul is in tumult;
my heart is poured out in grief
    because of the destruction of the daughter of my
        people,
because infants and babes faint
    in the streets of the city.

¹²They cry to their mothers,
    "Where is bread and wine?"
as they faint like wounded men
    in the streets of the city,
as their life is poured out
    on their mothers' bosom.

¹³What can I say for you, to what compare you,
    O daughter of Jerusalem?
What can I liken to you, that I may comfort you,
    O virgin daughter of Zion?
For vast as the sea is your ruin;
    who can restore you?

¹⁴Your prophets have seen for you
    false and deceptive visions;
they have not exposed your iniquity
    to restore your fortunes,
but have seen for you oracles
    false and misleading.

¹⁵All who pass along the way
    clap their hands at you;
tney hiss and wag their heads
    at the daughter of Jerusalem;
"Is this the city which was called
    the perfection of beauty,
    the joy of all the earth?"

¹⁶All your enemies
    rail against you;
they hiss, they gnash their teeth,
    they cry: "We have destroyed her!
Ah, this is the day we longed for;
    now we have it; we see it!"

¹⁷The LORD has done what he purposed,
    has carried out his threat;
as he ordained long ago,
    he has demolished without pity;
he has made the enemy rejoice over you.
    and exalted the might of your foes.

The first part of the poem goes into great detail spelling out the theme of divine causality alluded to in Chapter One: the fall of Jerusalem is the Lord's doing; it is not an arbitrary punishment, but the fulfillment of a warning. Yahweh is faithful to bad promises as well as good; so much so that he is willing to destroy the "splendor of Israel, . . . his footstool" (v.1), his beloved Zion and the Temple where he had chosen to dwell. The poet does not doubt God's love, though, or his desire to restore and save; otherwise there would be no point in prayer. Hell, says novelist Flannery

O'Connor, is a sign that God takes us seriously. The destruction of Jerusalem for infidelity is a sign that Yahweh takes his covenant seriously.

The downfall of Jerusalem is described as a fall from heaven, from absolute height, to earth (v.1). The Temple seemed to be indestructible, especially permanent because of Yahweh's promise to David (2 Sam 7:8-16). Now the people must realize that the visible Temple was a sign of the more profound reality of God's fidelity; but when it did not symbolize the same kind of fidelity on the side of the people, even the Temple was expendable. A church building, even the organization of people into a community, can become an end in itself and an empty symbol of the reality it is supposed to serve. Then it is better if the externals, with their false sense of security, are toppled. The Temple is called by the familiar names "tent," "altar," "sanctuary" (vv.4,7), but in verse 6 it is identified by the unaccustomed word "booth," a word that implies the fragility of the Temple. The comparison is to the makeshift shelter of a harvester that is knocked down after the harvest is complete.

Now, what seemed incomprehensible has happened: the Temple of Yahweh lies in ruins. Cultic life, once so vibrant, has ceased. The feasts are celebrated there no more. In place of the proud hymns of the people are heard the clamor of Israel's destroyers and the taunts of her enemies (v.7). In the final verse of the poem, a vivid contrast is drawn between the pilgrims of the past and the terrors of the present (v.22). A festival of joy has been replaced by a lament of bitterness.

The defeat of the strongholds and the fall of the kingdom (v.2) call to mind the historical events leading up to the deportation. The armies of Babylon destroyed many of the cities in the Jerusalem area on the way to capturing the citadel, even attacking the fortified cities of Judah (Jer 34:7). In 598 B.C., King Jehoiakim, a son of the reforming king, Josiah, had been deposed. He had played politics under siege and been in harsh disagreement with the prophet Jeremiah. His own son, Jehoiachin, was installed in his place but three months later removed to Babylon Jehoiakim's brother Zedekiah was then made king in Jerusalem. Zedekiah was weak and vacillating and fell victim to the intrigues around him. He was persuaded to rebel against the Babylonians; when they came for the final suppression of Jerusalem in 587, Zedekiah was captured while trying to escape. He was made to witness the execution of his sons; then he was blinded and taken in chains to Babylon (2 Kgs 25:5-7).

In all this, Yahweh is seen as the agent of punishment. It is not the Babylonians who are in command, but Yahweh. The architect of the city oversees her dismantling. He carefully marked out the buildings and the walks that would be broken down (v.8). He cut down the might of Israel (or, in the original, "lopped off the horns of Israel"), withdrawing his "right hand," which protected the people. He destroyed everything, even the walls and gates surrounding her.

Besides the kings, Zion has lost the ministers, priests and prophets central to her life under God's care. High tragedy is exposed in the understatement: "The *torah* is no more" (v.9). The elders perform the mourning rites for the city as for a dead person: sitting on the ground in a posture of humiliation, covering their heads with dirt in a gesture symbolizing the end of all mortals (v.10). The maidens are mentioned in the same breath with the elders: perhaps these two extremes of the population are meant to indicate that everyone in the city is mourning. The foundations of faith seem to be lost forever: Temple, Law, prophet and priest are gone.

Unlike the passerby of Chapter One, the narrator here is personally involved: "My eyes are spent with weeping" (v.11). He speaks of the fallen city with great tenderness, even while recognizing her guilt. Eleven times he calls her "daughter": daughter of Zion, daughter of Jerusalem, daughter of Jacob. With great emotion he addresses her

directly in verse 13: "O daughter!," comparing her ruin to
the vastness of the sea. She has been misled by false prophets
and is even now taunted by enemies who think that it is they
who are responsible for her downfall (v.16). They hiss at
her as Jeremiah promised they would (v.15; Jer 19:8; 25:9).
Meanwhile her babies are dying of starvation (vv.11-12).

LET TEARS STREAM DOWN
2:18-22

¹⁸Cry aloud to the Lord!
    O daughter of Zion!
Let tears stream down like a torrent
    day and night!
Give yourself no rest,
    your eyes no respite!

¹⁹Arise, cry out in the night,
    at the beginning of the watches!
Pour out your heart like water
    before the presence of the Lord!
Lift your hands to him
    for the lives of your children,
who faint for hunger
    at the head of every street.

²⁰Look, O LORD, and see!
    With whom hast thou dealt thus?
Should women eat their offspring,
    the children of their tender care?
Should priest and prophet be slain
    in the sanctuary of the Lord?
²¹In the dust of the streets
    lie the young and the old;
my maidens and my young men
    have fallen by the sword;
in the day of thy anger thou hast slain them,
    slaughtering without mercy.

> 22Thou didst invite as to the day of an appointed feast
> my terrors on every side;
> and on the day of the anger of the LORD
> none escaped or survived;
> those whom I dandled and reared
> my enemy destroyed.

The only remedy is recourse to the Lord. The poet urges Jerusalem to turn her weeping into prayer: "Pour out your heart like water before the presence of the Lord!" (v.19). No one but the Lord can reverse her fortunes. It has taken the extreme agony of the invasion to convince Jerusalem of her sinfulness and dependence on Yahweh. Pride always blocks true knowledge of self and a true assessment of the place that God should occupy in one's life. It often takes unrelieved tragedy to bring us to our knees. There is a danger of selfishness even here; to transcend this, Jerusalem is urged to center her prayer on the lives of her children (v.19).

Verses 20-22 should be read as the prayer of Jerusalem herself. "Look, O Lord," of verse 20 in this poem corresponds to the same invocation in verse 20 of the first chapter. God's attention is directed to the abominations of the siege of Jerusalem: cannibalism; murder of the ministers in the very sanctuary where they served; slaughter of old and young in the streets (Deut 28:53; Jer 19:9). The new generation, the hope of the future, has been cut down in the flower of youth. Jerusalem makes her own the ironic comparison of verse 7: the traditional feast day has become a day of wrath (v.22).

THIRD LAMENTATION

THE POEM IN CHAPTER THREE is the center of the book; this focus is stressed by the intricacy of its alphabetic acrostic. Each letter of the alphabet begins three lines instead of one. Verses one, two, and three, for example, each begin with the first letter, Aleph (A); four, five, and six with Beth (B); and so forth to the end of the alphabet. The spokesman here is a "man who has seen affliction" (v. 1), but at times words seem to come from the city herself (vv.52-63). The lamentation is expressing the pain of an average citizen of Jerusalem, or of the citizens as a corporate group. In a more universal sense, this poem expresses the intense suffering of any believer who feels beaten down by tragedy, which however is perceived as the just judgment of God. The poem falls into two main parts, a description of the misery (vv.1-39), and a description of the sufferer's response to it (vv.40-66). Each of these sections has an evident subdivision, as will be pointed out.

DARKNESS AND LIGHT
3:1-39

> 3 I am the man who has seen affliction
> under the rod of his wrath;
> ²he has driven and brought me
> into darkness without any light;
> ³surely against me he turns his hand
> again and again the whole day long.

⁴He has made my flesh and my skin waste away,
   and broken my bones;
⁵he has besieged and enveloped me
   with bitterness and tribulation;
⁶he has made me dwell in darkness
   like the dead of long ago.

⁷He has walled me about so that I cannot escape;
   he has put heavy chains on me;
⁸though I call and cry for help,
   he shuts out my prayer;
⁹he has blocked my ways with hewn stones,
   he has made my paths crooked.

¹⁰He is to me like a bear lying in wait,
   like a lion in hiding;
¹¹he led me off my way and tore me to pieces;
   he has made me desolate;
¹²he bent his bow and set me
   as a mark for his arrow.

¹³He drove into my heart
   the arrows of his quiver;
¹⁴I have become the laughingstock of all peoples,
   the burden of their songs all day long.
¹⁵He has filled me with bitterness,
   he has sated me with wormwood.

¹⁶He has made my teeth grind on gravel,
   and made me cower in ashes;
¹⁷my soul is bereft of peace,
   I have forgotten what happiness is;
¹⁸so I say, "Gone is my glory,
   and my expectation from the LORD."

¹⁹Remember my affliction and my bitterness,
   the wormwood and the gall!
²⁰My soul continually thinks of it
   and is bowed down within me.
²¹But this I call to mind,
   and therefore I have hope:

²²The steadfast love of the LORD never ceases,
   his mercies never come to an end;
²³they are new every morning;
   great is thy faithfulness.
²⁴"The LORD is my portion," says my soul,
   "therefore I will hope in him."

²⁵The LORD is good to those who wait for him,
   to the soul that seeks him.
²⁶It is good that one should wait quietly
   for the salvation of the LORD.
²⁷It is good for a man that he bear the yoke in his youth.

²⁸Let him sit alone in silence
   when he has laid it on him;
²⁹let him put his mouth in the dust—
   there may yet be hope;
³⁰let him give his cheek to the smiter,
   and be filled with insults.

³¹For the Lord will not
   cast off for ever,
³²but, though he cause grief, he will have compassion
   according to the abundance of his steadfast love;
³³for he does not willingly afflict
   or grieve the sons of men.

³⁴To crush under foot
   all the prisoners of the earth,
³⁵to turn aside the right of a man
   in the presence of the Most High,
³⁶to subvert a man in his cause,
   the Lord does not approve.

³⁷Who has commanded and it came to pass,
   unless the Lord has ordained it?
³⁸Is it not from the mouth of the Most High
   that good and evil come?
³⁹Why should a living man complain,
   a man, about the punishment of his sins?

The poet begins by describing himself as a prisoner or slave under the rod of a cruel master. God here is anything but the Good Shepherd. His "right hand" has been withdrawn from its protecting position (2:3) and has instead been turned against the suppliant. The experience is not momentary: the darkness is not only that of the dead, but of the long dead (v.6). It is like being in a prison of chains and heavy stones. Even spiritual escape is blocked: "He shuts out my prayer" (v.8). This extravagant language about God's insensitivity to the prayer of the sufferer is typical of the Old Testament (Job 19:7; 30:20; Jer 11:11); he "hides his face" from the seeker (Isa 1:15; 59:2).

In this first part there is a picture of unrelieved misery and pessimism which, if it stood alone, would surely make us conclude to the despair of the complainer who has been driven to extremes by his experience of God as hostile and merciless. Yahweh is like a bear or a lion (v.10); he has torn me to pieces (v.12), shot arrows at me and brought in enemies to taunt me (vv.13-15). The poet is so overwhelmed by suffering that he can say "I have forgotten what happiness is" (v.17). When suffering or sickness becomes drawn out, throbbing, endless, it seems to engulf everything, to affect one's total view of reality. This suffering is all there is. One cannot even remember or visualize what it would be like not to be suffering. This is the ultimate test of faith in a God of love. It is the experience of the end of hope: "Gone is my expectation from the Lord" (v.18).

Then comes the great surprise, almost a *creatio ex nihilo*: "Therefore I have hope: the steadfast love of the Lord never ceases" (vv.21-22). Verse 21 is transitional to the following section, a link from despair to hope. The poet reaches down into the deep well of his faith for this statement of hope based on God's love. There is nothing in his present experience to validate this faith: it is based on his knowledge and experience of God before this tragedy. Anyone who suffers has to reach beyond the present sadness to the current of faith and hope running underneath. Paul described the patriarch Abraham as "hoping against hope" (Rom 4:18 NAB). The believer knows that the Lord's mercy is "new every morning" (v.23); it is always present because the Lord is faithful, but it is experienced in continually different ways. That it is not felt now is not proof that his love is absent nor that it will not be felt again.

What recourse does the believer have in such circumstances? Faith leads one to hope, and hope makes it possible to wait for the Lord to act: "It is good that one should wait quietly for the salvation of the Lord" (v.26). Wait in silence and with complete humility before the one who is master of all. Kissing or licking the dust (v.29) was a sign of extreme obeisance in the Ancient Near East. The attitude called for is one of complete abandonment to God's will. The sufferer humbles himself, letting it all depend on God.

Because the believer has a deep knowledge of the Lord, even unrelieved misery cannot seem endless. Yahweh does not take pleasure in inflicting pain (v.33). When he punishes it is remedial: to elicit sorrow for sin and turn the sinner back to him. This punishment, the poet repeats, is not accidental; it is from the Lord, the creator of all. The reason for it cannot be seen by the sufferer, but it has a purpose in God's plan.

JUDGE AND REDEEMER
3:40-66

> 40Let us test and examine our ways,
>   and return to the LORD!
> 41Let us lift up our hearts and hands
>   to God in heaven:
> 42"We have transgressed and rebelled,
>   and thou hast not forgiven.
>
> 43"Thou hast wrapped thyself with anger and pursued us,
>   slaying without pity;

⁴⁴thou hast wrapped thyself with a cloud
   so that no prayer can pass through.
⁴⁵Thou hast made us offscouring and refuse
   among the peoples.

⁴⁶"All our enemies
   rail against us;
⁴⁷panic and pitfall have come upon us,
   devastation and destruction;
⁴⁸my eyes flow with rivers of tears
   because of the destruction of the daughter of my
     people.

⁴⁹"My eyes will flow without ceasing, without respite,
⁵⁰until the LORD from heaven
   looks down and sees;·
⁵¹my eyes cause me grief
   at the fate of all the maidens of my city.

⁵²"I have been hunted like a bird
   by those who were my enemies without cause;
⁵³they flung me alive into the pit
   and cast stones on me;
⁵⁴water closed over my head;
   I said, 'I am lost.'

⁵⁵"I called on thy name, O LORD,
   from the depths of the pit;
⁵⁶thou didst hear my plea, 'Do not close
   thine ear to my cry for help!'
⁵⁷Thou didst come near when I called on thee;
   thou didst say, 'Do not fear!'

⁵⁸"Thou hast taken up my cause, O Lord,
   thou hast redeemed my life.
⁵⁹Thou hast seen the wrong done to me, O LORD;
   judge thou my cause.
⁶⁰Thou hast seen all their vengeance, all
   their devices against me.

61"Thou hast heard their taunts, O LORD,
all their devices against me.
62The lips and thoughts of my assailants
are against me all the day long.
63Behold their sitting and their rising;
I am the burden of their songs.

64"Thou wilt requite them, O LORD,
according to the work of their hands.
65Thou wilt give them dullness of heart;
thy curse will be on them.
66Thou wilt pursue them in anger and destroy them
from under thy heavens, O LORD."

The response of the sufferer to chastisement by the Lord begins with a call to prayer: "Return to the Lord!" (v.40). Note the use of the first person plural in verses 40-47; more clearly than elsewhere, here the poet speaks in the name of the community. In verse 55 the mood changes to confidence that the prayer has been heard and will be answered favorably. The divine response will be redemption of the sufferer and just retribution for his enemies.

The accusing tone of verses 43-45 jars with the immediate context. It seems to belong with the section before verse 21, where God's hostility to Jerusalem and her people was the subject. Here the accusation is no less graphic: you wrapped yourself in anger, slayed without pity; no prayer can come through your self-imposed shield (see v.8). The mention of the "cloud" (v.44) may spark a mental connection for today's Christian reader with the spiritual masterpiece of an English writer of the 14th century, *The Cloud Of Unknowing*. The "cloud of unknowing," however, is not impenetrable by prayer. In fact, it is precisely the prayer of faith that finds God unerringly like an arrow from a well-aimed bow. Though the image is the same, its pessimistic use in Lamentations is the opposite of its use by the author of *The Cloud*. The figure does not tell the whole story in Lamentations, either: these verses begin the direct address to God that will govern the remainder of this lament; they are the harsh launching pad of a prayer that ends in confidence.

The mention of the pit in verses 53-57 was one of the reasons that supported the author's identification with the prophet Jeremiah. Jeremiah had been cast into a cistern because of his prediction of the fall of Jerusalem and his call for peaceful surrender and cooperation with the captors (Jer 38:1-13). The pit and the water, however, are traditional symbols for helplessness in the midst of suffering (Pss 40:3; 69:2,15; Job 22:11; Isa 30:28; Jonah 2:4,6). The poet resorts to these well-known images, as well as many others, to portray the anguish of city and people.

The plea for God's attention ("Look, O Lord!") that was noted toward the end of the first two lamentations appears here again, but in more muted tones (v.50). Perhaps the reason is that confidence in a divine hearing is more strongly expressed in this third chapter. We have noticed an alternation between hopeless affliction (vv.1-20) and hopeful prayer (vv.21-41) in the first section; the bitterness reappears in the second part (vv.42-54), but the hope comes back in verse 55, which sounds the keynote for the final section: "Thou didst come near when I called on thee; thou didst say, 'Do not fear'!" (v.57).

But the last thought in the chapter is a plea for retribution. Like Job, the sufferer here asks for God to be his witness (Job 16:19; 19:25); nothing is hidden from God (v.59). The poet feels persecuted by his enemies in both "their sitting" and "their rising," which means all the time, resting or working. The request for vengeance disappoints those who have heard Jesus forgive his persecutors from the cross. This seems to lower the pitch of the magnificent poem right at the end. But the revelation of love in Christ had not been given when this was written. The imagery could be used by New Testament writers and the Christian liturgy to describe Jesus' suffering. But Jesus gave a new meaning to suffering not foreseen in Lamentations.

FOURTH LAMENTATION

AFTER THE DEPTHS of bitterness and the heights of hope of Chapter Three, the Fourth Lamentation is an emotional letdown. The pain is still severe, but the statement is a little more objective. Jerusalem herself does not speak. At first the voice seems to be that of a reporter, but eventually this reporter is one who has experienced the tragedy of the city (vv.17-20). The theme of "tragic reversal" is taken up from Chapters One and Two, where it focused on the city as a whole, and is here described of various inhabitants. Up till now there have been three lines of poetry for each letter of the Hebrew alphabet (in Chapters One and Two, only the first of these three lines begins with the pertinent letter; in Chapter Three all three lines are "alphabetized"); in Chapter Four, this diminishes to two lines, and in the Fifth, to one. Perhaps this is a poetic way of indicating that the height of passion has been reached in the central poem; now all that remains is dogged perseverance in suffering until relief comes. The end of the Exile is foreseen and spoken of for the first time (v.22).

THE FALLEN STONES
4:1-10

> **4** How the gold has grown dim,
>   how the pure gold is changed!
> The holy stones lie scattered
>   at the head of every street.

²The precious sons of Zion,
   worth their weight in fine gold,
how they are reckoned as earthen pots,
   the work of a potter's hands!

³Even the jackals give the breast
   and suckle their young,
but the daughter of my people has become cruel,
   like the ostriches in the wilderness.

⁴The tongue of the nursling cleaves
   to the roof of its mouth for thirst;
the children beg for food,
   but no one gives to them.

⁵Those who feasted on dainties
   perish in the streets;
those who were brought up in purple
lie on ash heaps.

⁶For the chastisement of the daughter
   of my people has been greater
than the punishment of Sodom,
which was overthrown in a moment,
   no hand being laid on it.

⁷Her princes were purer than snow,
   whiter than milk;
their bodies were more ruddy than coral,
   the beauty of their form was like sapphire.

⁸Now their visage is blacker than soot,
   they are not recognized in the streets;
their skin has shriveled upon their bones,
   it has become as dry as wood.

⁹Happier were the victims of the sword
   than the victims of hunger,
who pined away, stricken
   by want of the fruits of the field.

¹⁰The hands of compassionate women
  have boiled their own children;
they became their food
  in the destruction of the daughter of my people.

The "gold" of Jerusalem at the beginning of this lamentation might be the temple treasure, and the "stones" might be its fallen walls. Verse 2 reveals that these treasures are really the city's inhabitants. We are on the way to the idea of the "living stones" of 1 Peter 2; and to the story of Saint Lawrence, who, when asked to present the treasures of the Church, brought together the sick and the poor. There will always be much illusion surrounding what people treasure (Mt 6:19-24).

Again the horror of Jerusalem's downfall is described by the fate of the most vulnerable of her inhabitants, the infants (vv.3-4). Jerusalem is "cruel," even worse than the ostrich, who was believed to be so insensitive to the needs of her offspring that she left her eggs in the sand to be trampled or eaten.

"The wings of the ostrich wave proudly;
  but are they the pinions and plumage of
  love?" (Job 39:13)

Perhaps the willingness of mothers to behave like cannibals toward their own babies is a sign of the malady that caused the downfall of the city: the people didn't realize, as they worshiped and observed the externals of the law, that just underneath the surface was a moral vacuum. The adjective "compassionate" in verse 10 is meant ironically. It is a commonplace that tragedy uncovers the priorities and values that actually govern people's lives. In the suddenness of fire, flood or storm, people may reveal themselves as looters or selfless heroes.

The rich have become destitute; strong, healthy princes have become weak and dirty (vv.5-8). "Lying on ash heaps" should bring to mind the story of Job and his reversals of fortune (Job 2:8). Like Job, many of the inhabitants of

Jerusalem are innocent. The poet wonders why Jerusalem must suffer a slow agonizing punishment at the hand of a cruel invader, when Sodom, the paradigm of the wicked city, received a quick and relatively painless sentence directly from the hand of God (v.6). "Happier were the victims of the sword than the victims of hunger" (v.9).

THE LORD HIMSELF HAS SCATTERED THEM
4:11-22

> ¹¹The LORD gave full vent to his wrath,
>   he poured out his hot anger;
> and he kindled a fire in Zion,
>   which consumed its foundations.

> ¹²The kings of the earth did not believe,
>   or any of the inhabitants of the world,
> that foe or enemy could enter
>   the gates of Jerusalem.

> ¹³This was for the sins of her prophets
>   and the iniquities of her priests,
> who shed in the midst of her
>   the blood of the righteous.

> ¹⁴They wandered, blind, through the streets,
>   so defiled with blood
> that none could touch
>   their garments.

> ¹⁵"Away! Unclean!" men cried at them;
>   "Away! Away! Touch not!"
> So they became fugitives and wanderers;
>   men said among the nations,
>   "They shall stay with us no longer."

> ¹⁶The LORD himself has scattered them,
>   he will regard them no more;
> no honor was shown to the priests,
>   no favor to the elders.

17Our eyes failed, ever watching
   vainly for help;
in our watching we watched
   for a nation which could not save.

18Men dogged our steps
   so that we could not walk in our streets;
our end drew near; our days were numbered;
   for our end had come.

19Our pursuers were swifter
   than the vultures in the heavens;
they chased us on the mountains,
   they lay in wait for us in the wilderness.

20The breath of our nostrils, the LORD'S anointed,
   was taken in their pits,
he of whom we said, "Under his shadow
   we shall live among the nations."

21Rejoice and be glad, O daughter of Edom,
   dweller in the land of Uz;
but to you also the cup shall pass;
   you shall become drunk and strip yourself bare.

22The punishment of your iniquity, O daughter of
      Zion, is accomplished,
   he will keep you in exile no longer;
but your iniquity, O daughter of Edom, he will punish,
   he will uncover your sins.

The divine causality of Jerusalem's fall present in every poem and mentioned obliquely earlier in this one (v.6) is now given clear expression in the second half of the Fourth Lamentation. The destruction and exile was the result of the Lord's anger (v.11), in answer to the sins of her prophets and priests (v.13); he was capable of punishing Jerusalem, and he will punish her hostile neighbors when the time comes (vv.21-22). Again the image of fire expresses God's chastisement (see 1:13; 2:3).

The impregnability of Jerusalem was a proverb among the Hebrews (1 Kgs 8:12-13; 2 Kgs 19:32-34; Ps 132:13-14). Because of its natural setting it had been a strong military base long before David had captured it by stealth (2 Sam 5:6-7; 1 Chr 11:5). But more than this the people relied on the promise of Yahweh that his covenant, represented by the city and temple, would not be forsaken. This confident attitude of the Hebrew people is projected to the whole world: no one believed Jerusalem could be taken (v.12). The infidelity of the people was due especially to the false leadership of the priests and prophets. The prophets have been condemned for this before (2:14), but this is the first time the priests have been singled out. They are pictured as having wandered like blind lepers through the ruined streets of Jerusalem (vv.14-15). Now they have been "scattered" by the Lord (v.16). As another evidence that God brings unexpected good out of tragedy, even sin and its punishment, we remark that it was the priests in exile who were mainly responsible for the collection, editing and writing of the books of the Old Testament.

Pointed historical connections are the burden of verses 17-20. Many of the inhabitants of Jerusalem, misled by their priests and prophets and king, looked to Egypt for salvation from the invading Babylonians. The Egyptians did for a time distract the Babylonians (Jer 37:5), causing a momentary revolt by the Jerusalem leaders, but Egypt withdrew, proving to be a "nation which could not save" (v.17). In retaliation the Babylonians were harsh in dealing with the Jerusalem leaders, pursuing King Zedekiah, blinding him and taking him off into exile. As the successor of David, the king was looked on as the "Lord's anointed" (*messiah*). The king is also described in an ancient formula used by both Egyptians and Canaanites: "the breath of our nostrils" (v.20), though the Israelite idea of kingship was not so linked to divine prerogative as among those peoples. In Egypt the king was a god, Horus. His divine power reached the nation through the human monarch. In Mesopotamia the gods gave kingship to the people; the human king was their representative. He transmitted divine decisions (arrived at with the help of a council) and even took the place of the god in the spring festival.

As in the First and Third Lamentations, the Fourth ends with an appeal for retribution on enemies. The Edomites are specified. They applauded the downfall of Jerusalem and took advantage of the Hebrews' plight for personal gain. This spiteful act, added to the traditional hatred between the two nations, deepened a wound that would never be completely healed (see Ps 137). If nations had categorized each other in our terms as "most favored nation" and so forth, Israel would certainly have tagged Edom "most hated neighbor." Obadiah devotes much of his prophecy to gloating over Edom's downfall at a later time [See Commentary later in this volume]. Much to our surprise after descriptions of unrelieved disaster in the earlier part of Lamentations, the poet foresees the end of the Exile approaching (v.22); in the same breath he warns Edom that her time is coming.

FIFTH LAMENTATION

THE FIFTH LAMENTATION is the shortest of the five. Though it is not alphabetical, it has twenty-two verses like the others, but only one line for each verse. It is different in other ways, too. It begins as a direct address to the Lord rather than with the dirge-like complaints of the other poems. The speaker is not the city or an individual, but the people as a group. The different nature of this chapter was noticed by early translators. It was entitled "The Prayer of Jeremiah" in the Latin Vulgate and "A Prayer" in some of the Greek versions.

The poet describes for the Lord in summary form the disgrace of Jerusalem as seen by her people. The status of "orphans and widows" (v.3) refers to the defenseless situation of all the inhabitants after the destruction, but it may also imply that many of the male Hebrews perished in the defense of the city and Temple. The idea of "inheritance" relates this condition to the more spiritual notion of abandonment by Yahweh. They have lost not only homes and city, but what God had promised them. The prayer subtly implies that God cannot forget his responsibility for their plight; and to prove himself faithful must restore them. This will be the plea which climaxes this poem and the book in verses 21-22.

JACKALS ON MOUNT ZION
5:1-18

5 Remember, O LORD, what has befallen us;
  behold, and see our disgrace!
²Our inheritance has been turned over to strangers,
  our homes to aliens.
³We have become orphans, fatherless;
  our mothers are like widows.
⁴We must pay for the water we drink,
  the wood we get must be bought.
⁵With a yoke on our necks we are hard driven;
  we are weary, we are given no rest.
⁶We have given the hand to Egypt,
  and to Assyria, to get bread enough.
⁷Our fathers sinned, and are no more;
  and we bear their iniquities.
⁸Slaves rule over us;
  there is none to deliver us from their hand.
⁹We get our bread at the peril of our lives,
  because of the sword in the wilderness.
¹⁰Our skin is hot as an oven
  with the burning heat of famine.
¹¹Women are ravished in Zion,
  virgins in the towns of Judah.
¹²Princes are hung up by their hands;
  no respect is shown to the elders.
¹³Young men are compelled to grind at the mill;
  and boys stagger under loads of wood.
¹⁴The old men have quit the city gate,
  the young men their music.
¹⁵The joy of our hearts has ceased;
  our dancing has been turned to mourning.
¹⁶The crown has fallen from our head;
  woe to us, for we have sinned!

¹⁷For this our heart has become sick,
  for these things our eyes have grown dim,
¹⁸for Mount Zion which lies desolate;
  jackals prowl over it.

Now natives of Judah must pay for the basics of life which once belonged to them or were easily accessible from community sources (v.4). They are weary from the struggle merely to survive; but the plaint "We are given no rest" (v.5) goes deeper than this. They had been promised a place of rest from the Exodus onward, and through the wandering in the desert. The rest has been taken away. In fact, from the perspective of the author of the Letter to the Hebrews, they never achieved the "rest" of the Lord in the proper sense. Complacency had been mistaken for the rest of the Lord and given rise to disobedience. This is at least a different slant on the kind of sinfulness which led to Jerusalem's downfall. The same complacency can stymie any of us: "While the promise of entering his rest remains, let us fear lest any of you be judged to have failed to reach it . . . . Let us therefore strive to enter that rest, that no one fall by the same sort of disobedience" (Heb 4:1,11).

The reference to Egypt and to Assyria, the region in Mesopotamia north of Babylon (v.6), may be a way of pointing out the irony that the alliances the Israelites sought earlier in spite of prophetic instruction have come back to haunt them in their time of need. Now they must go to the same countries seeking the fundamental necessities of life. Even though the Lord does not strike us with lightning bolts when we act contrary to his will, our sins have a way of visiting us again in their unforeseen consequences. The poet seems to blame the punishment of Jerusalem on earlier generations (v.7), an attitude reflected in Jeremiah (31:29) and Ezekiel (18:1-2). But the prophets correct or complete the idea of collective guilt with their teaching of individual responsibility. In the same way, later in the Fifth Lamentation personal guilt is admitted (v.16).

The "slaves" ruling in Jerusalem are the Babylonian officials appointed by the foreign power to rule in Judah. They are subordinates, a sad contrast to the divinely sanctioned kings who ruled Israel: "The crown has fallen from our head" (v.16). Life in these new conditions is a battle for survival. All levels of Hebrew society are degraded; women, princes, elders, young men, old men. Grinding at the mill (v.13) was considered a menial task left to the weak and to slaves and prisoners, a job demeaning to strong young men. The excitement has gone out of the life of the people. Mount Zion, formerly the center of liturgy and life, is so ruined and abandoned that wild animals prowl over it unmolested (v.18).

RESTORE US, O LORD!
5:19-22

> [19]But thou, O LORD, dost reign for ever;
>   thy throne endures to all generations.
> [20]Why dost thou forget us for ever,
>   why dost thou so long forsake us?
> [21]Restore us to thyself, O LORD, that we
>   may be restored!
>   Renew our days as of old!
> [22]Or hast thou utterly rejected us?
>   Art thou exceedingly angry with us?

The poet's faith sees a reality beyond the scene before his eyes. Yahweh is not dead, as the taunting invaders and hostile neighbors insist. He reigns forever. The Temple, his earthly footstool (2:1), is gone, but his heavenly throne is eternal (v.19). Part of the problem with Israelite religion during the century before the Babylonian massacre had been a too cross identification of Yahweh with his material Temple in Jerusalem (Jer 7:2-7). Here we sense the beginning of a purified and more exalted notion of Yahweh that will be one of the best fruits of the Exile. In Babylon the exiles came to realize that Yahweh was still active and powerful in their lives, that the destruction of his Temple had not been a defeat for him, but part of his own plan. He was not limited to Israel, but also reigned in Babylon. The prophets of the Exile helped the Israelites move to an understanding of God's transcendence (Isa 46:9; 51:12-16; Ezek 1:26-28; 10).

The collapse of the city and the onslaught of the Exile also brought to the chosen people a deep sense of humility. Their prophets had told them over and over to be dependent on the Lord, but they had come to think that he had made himself dependent on them because of his own covenant promises. This illusion was wiped away in suffering. Restoration will not come about by the action of the people, but only by divine intervention: restore us, Lord, renew us!—for we cannot renew ourselves (v.21).

Bibliography

P. R. Ackroyd, *Exile and Restoration: A Study of Hebrew Thought of the Sixth Century B. C.* (Old Testament Library). Philadelphia: Westminster Press, 1968. Pages 1-61.

W. J. Fuerst, *The Books of Ruth, Esther, Ecclesiastes, The Song of Songs, Lamentations: The Five Scrolls* (Cambridge Bible Commentary). Cambridge and New York: Cambridge University Press, 1975.

N. K. Gottwald, "Book of Lamentations," *Interpreter's Bible* (1962), Volume 3, pages 61-63.

N. K. Gottwald, *Studies in the Book of Lamentations* (Studies in Biblical Theology, 14), London: SCM, 1959.

D. R. Hillers, *Lamentations* (Anchor Bible, 7A). Garden City: Doubleday, 1972.

G. T. Montague, *The Books of Zephaniah, Nahum, Habakkuk, Lamentations, Obadiah* (Old Testament Reading Guide, 19). Collegeville: Liturgical Press, 1967. Pages 63-97.

Haggai

HAGGAI

The Prophet

HAGGAI THE PROPHET had a major role to play in the life of the Jewish community newly returned from exile in Babylon. It was brief and limited, but important. During four months in 520 B.C., he roused the people out of their lethargy to finish the rebuilding of the Temple. They had laid the foundations soon after the return from the Exile in 538 B.C., but in the struggle to settle their families, build their own homes, and protect themselves against hostile neighbors, the returnees had lost their sense of urgency for the restoration of the Temple. Haggai and his contemporary, Zechariah the prophet, issued a call to action. These two are linked in the national memory (Ezra 5:1; 6:14) whether or not they considered themselves co-workers. What is said here as background to Haggai's work will hold for Zechariah as well.

Of Haggai himself we know very little, in fact only the information provided by the collection of four oracles that bear his name. According to this source, he began speaking out on the matter of the Temple in the sixth month (August-September) of 520, and made his final statement in the ninth month (November-December) of the same year.

History

Babylon, the Eastern power which had brought about Israel's downfall in 587 B.C., met her own nemesis in 539 in the person of Cyrus the Great, founder of the Persian Empire. An anonymous prophet of the Exile had seen the handwriting on the wall when Cyrus began his assault on Babylon and her neighbors a few years before. Second Isaiah painted Cyrus as the deliverer of God's people, even going so far as to describe the pagan king as the Lord's "anointed" (*messiah*: Isa 45:1). Cyrus proved a disappointment to the prophet in some ways, but his main prediction was correct: the victory of Cyrus over Babylon would mean the release of the Hebrews from exile. In 538 Cyrus issued a decree permitting Jews confined in Babylon to return to Jerusalem to rebuild the city and the Temple (Ezra 1:1-4). This was in line with general Persian policy. The Persians were generally very tolerant toward the religious institutions of their subject peoples. They encouraged and even supported these religions in the interests of building good will and at the same time exercising control.

For the same reason the Persians were willing to appoint local rulers from the ranks of the subject peoples. For the return to Jerusalem. Cyrus chose Sheshbazzar as leader and first governor. Though he has a Babylonian name, Sheshbazzar is described as a "prince of Judah" (Ezra 1:8). It was natural for the Jews living in Mesopotámia for a generation to be gradually acculturated to the life of Babylon, including the adoption of Babylonian names. Sheshbazzar's successor also had a Babylonian name, Zerubbabel. These two leaders, by the way, became confused in the records that have come down to us; probably, most scholars feel, because later editors sometimes inserted the name of Zerubbabel for that of Sheshbazzar, in order to highlight the career of Zerubbabel, who was the great-grandson of the beloved King Josiah and thus a direct link with the glories of pre-exilic Jerusalem.

Sheshbazzar was given the Temple vessels that had been taken from Jerusalem in 587 along with his instructions to rebuild the Temple on the original site (Ezra 5:14-15). The work began immediately on their return in 538; first, the altar of holocausts was set up and the practice of sacrificing to Yahweh reinstituted; then within the year the foundations of the Temple were begun (Ezra 3:1-11).

Soon, however, the opposition of Judah's neighbors was aroused, along with that of some of the aliens who had come into the area while the Jews were in exile. According to the report in the Book of Ezra (4:1-24), the Samaritans wrote to the Persian ruler, complaining that the plan to rebuild the Temple amounted to an act of treason. The ruler responded by halting the work of reconstruction. No further progress was made during the next fifteen years. It was at this point that Haggai and Zechariah came on the scene.

In the meantime changes had taken place in the larger political arena. Rule in Persia had changed hands twice since the decree of Cyrus, who had been killed in battle in 529. He was succeeded by his son, Cambyses II, who broadened the empire to include Egypt while maintaining the same tolerant attitude toward subject peoples. After his death in 522, a pretender, Gaumata the Magian, posed as Cambyses' (murdered) brother and claimed the throne. The confusion and disturbance caused by this provoked a number of the subordinate states to revolt for independence. About the time Haggai and Zechariah began preaching, Darius, a member of the royal family, had been able to defeat Gaumata and to subdue the various revolutionaries, virtually consolidating his own power.

CHAPTER ONE

THE BEGINNING of Haggai's preaching campaign for the rebuilding of the Temple is very precisely dated to the first day of the sixth month of the second year of Darius (August-September, 520 B.C.). The prophet may have viewed the shakeup in the empire in the recent past as a sign of the approaching end of the age and the coming of the Day of Yahweh (Hag 2:6, 21-22) and high time to finish the building of the Temple. It is even more likely that he interpreted the revolts as a sign of the inner weakness and approaching dissolution of the empire and an opportunity for Judah herself to declare independence under the kingship of Zerubbabel (2:23).

It is to the two pillars of the new community that Haggai brings the word of the Lord: Zerubbabel, the governor, and Joshua, the high priest. They have impeccable credentials, Zerubbabel as the descendant of the last legitimate Davidic king, Joshua as a priest from a family that had served in the Solomonic Temple. Both had come from Babylon in the first wave of returnees.

A TIME TO BUILD
1:1-11

> **1** In the second year of Darius the king, in the sixth month, on the first day of the month, the word of the LORD came by Haggai the prophet to Zerubbabel the son of Shealtiel, governor of Judah, and to Joshua

the son of Jehozadak, the high priest, [2]"Thus says the LORD of hosts: This people say the time has not yet come to rebuild the house of the LORD." [3]Then the word of the LORD came by Haggai the prophet, [4]"Is it a time for you yourselves to dwell in your paneled houses, while this house lies in ruins? [5]Now therefore thus says the LORD of hosts: Consider how you have fared. [6]You have sown much, and harvested little; you eat, but you never have enough; you drink, but you never have your fill; you clothe yourselves, but no one is warm; and he who earns wages earns wages to put them into a bag with holes.

[7]"Thus says the LORD of hosts: Consider how you have fared. [8]Go up to the hills and bring wood and build the house, that I may take pleasure in it and that I may appear in my glory, says the LORD. [9]You have looked for much, and lo, it came to little; and when you brought it home, I blew it away. Why? says the LORD of hosts. Because of my house that lies in ruins, while you busy yourselves each with his own house. [10]Therefore the heavens above you have withheld the dew, and the earth has withheld its produce. [11]And I have called for a drought upon the land and the hills, upon the grain, the new wine, the oil, upon what the ground brings forth, upon men and cattle, and upon all their labors."

The message Haggai brings is very simple: it is time to finish the work of rebuilding the Temple. There is no call to reform stated, though an implicit call to faith and to a reorientation of priorities is involved. Why hasn't the Temple been built by now? According to the people, the time is not right (v.2). Their reason could be that they are not rich enough yet. Haggai turns the tables on them (v.6), declaring that the reason they have not prospered is their failure to attend to the Temple. Some scholars have pointed out the possibility that they are waiting for the literal fulfillment of Jeremiah's prophecy: "Thus says the Lord: 'When seventy years are completed for Babylon,

I will visit you, and I will fulfil to you my promise and bring you back to this place'" (Jer 29:10). Calculating from 587, there are still three years to go. Probably their hesitation was nothing this theological. The people had simply forgotten their dedication to the new Temple; after getting along without it for several years, they could think of many excuses for not rebuilding. When priorities fade a call to action is needed. The response the prophet received proves that his message struck home (v.14). When Pope John XXIII felt in his heart the inspiration to call Vatican Council II he knew it was the right time, but many others told him: "This is not the time." The Council took place and proved a challenge to the whole Church to hear Christian principles restated, to renew commitment to them, and to perform the action required. The word we already know and adhere to must be proclaimed again and again to call us back home, sometimes in small ways, sometimes with dramatic consequences like the restoration of the Temple.

The prophet chides the people for taking care of their own habitations while ignoring the needs of the Lord's house (vv.4,9). There is plenty of wood in the area, he says; you do not have to send to Lebanon for cedar as Solomon did, nor pay the high price he did (1 Kgs 5:1-12). There is no mention of stones because there are still plenty left from the ruined Temple and city. With the construction of the Temple there will be a suitable place for the glory of the Lord to dwell. In Ezekiel's vision, the glory of the Lord had departed from the destroyed Temple and would be coming to the renewed city to inhabit the new Temple (Ezek 11:22-23; 43:1-12).

I AM WITH YOU
1:12-15

12Then Zerubbabel the son of Shealtiel, and Joshua the son of Jehozadak, the high priest, with all the remnant of the people, obeyed the voice of the LORD their

God, and the words of Haggai the prophet, as the LORD their God had sent him; and the people feared before the LORD. ¹³Then Haggai, the messenger of the LORD, spoke to the people with the LORD'S message, "I am with you, says the LORD." ¹⁴And the LORD stirred up the spirit of Zerubbabel the son of Shealtiel, governor of Judah, and the spirit of Joshua the son of Jehozadak, the high priest, and the spirit of all the remnant of the people; and they came and worked on the house of the LORD of hosts, their God, ¹⁵on the twenty-fourth day of the month, in the sixth month.

The people are referred to as the "remnant," a term with messianic overtones used to describe those who remained faithful during trial and will be the basis of the new people. "A remnant will return, the remnant of Jacob, to the mighty God. For though your people Israel be as the sand of the sea, only a remnant of them will return" (Isa 10:21-22). The people addressed by Haggai have the marks of the true remnant, reverencing the Lord and obeying his word (v.12). Persecution and adversity have always been effective in removing the dead wood from God's community.

Haggai brings to the people the Lord's promise that has been bound up with his election and call throughout biblical history: "I am with you" (v.13). Jacob heard this (Gen 28:15), as did Moses (Ex 3:12), Gideon (6:16), Jeremiah (Jer 1:8), and Mary (Lk 1:28), to name a few. No other promise is necessary, and none else is as all-embracing, though anyone who is called wants to know more—the details—which is really less. The response of the community is positive. On the twenty-fourth day of the month the work of construction begins.

CHAPTER TWO

THREE MONTHS TO THE DAY after the work on the
Temple began, Haggai delivers his final oracles (2:10-19,
20-23). There is a certain completeness in this timing; it is
also a way of emphasizing the importance of the final utter-
ances, coming as they do on the anniversary of the inauguration of the rebuilding. Further, the second of the two last
oracles, the parting word, would naturally bear a message
the prophet wants remembered. This is exactly the way it is
here. The oracle to Zerubbabel climaxes the prophecy as
it recapitulates the overall message proclaimed by Haggai.
The oracle in verses 10-19, on the other hand, is repetitious
of the prophet's first preaching in Chapter One; some
scholars would even say that the oracle is out of its original
context, that "ninth month" has been changed from "sixth
month," and that these words belong to the day the work on
the Temple began (v.15).

But what about the intervening oracle (vv.1-9), which
comes on the twenty-first day of the seventh month? Why
does it break the pattern of the "twenty-fourth" day or why
isn't there an oracle for the twenty-first day of the eighth
month to complete the symmetry that is apparently in the
prophet's plan? There is a "hidden agenda" here that makes
this oracle the most significant of all.

THE FEAST OF BOOTHS
2:1-9

> **2**   In the second year of Darius the king, [1]in the seventh
> month, on the twenty-first day of the month, the word of

the LORD came by Haggai the prophet, [2]"Speak now to Zerubbabel the son of Shealtiel, governor of Judah, and to Joshua the son of Jehozadak, the high priest, and to all the remnant of the people, and say, [3]'Who is left among you that saw this house in its former glory? How do you see it now? Is it not in your sight as nothing? [4]Yet now take courage, O Zerubbabel, says the LORD; take courage, O Joshua, son of Jehozadak, the high priest; take courage, all you people of the land, says the LORD; work, for I am with you, says the LORD of hosts, [5]according to the promise that I made you when you came out of Egypt. My Spirit abides among you; fear not. [6]For thus says the LORD of hosts: Once again, in a little while, I will shake the heavens and the earth and the sea and the dry land; [7]and I will shake all nations, so that the treasures of all nations shall come in, and I will fill this house with splendor, says the LORD of hosts. [8]The silver is mine, and the gold is mine, says the LORD of hosts. [9]The latter splendor of this house shall be greater than the former, says the LORD of hosts; and in this place I will give prosperity, says the LORD of hosts.'"

The twenty-first day of the seventh month falls during the Feast of Booths or Tabernacles (Lev 23:34), a feast which would awaken deep religious and national emotion among the people. This had been the most popular feast of the year, because unlike the other two great feasts of Passover and Pentecost, it came at a time when harvesting was completed and all felt free to celebrate. This gave it the character of a national festival; originally, also, it was the feast marking the beginning of the year. Even more importantly for Haggai's program was the fact that Solomon's Temple had been dedicated during this feast (1 Kgs 8:2). The picture of people flocking to the Jerusalem Temple, as they did especially at Booths, became a standard image of the messianic kingdom in Hebrew prophecy (Isa 2:2-4; 56:6-7). Eventually the connection of messianic fulfillment to this feast became specific: "Then every one that survives of all the nations that have come against Jerusalem shall go up year after year to worship the King, the Lord of hosts, and to keep the feast of booths" (Zech 14:16).

In preaching to the leaders and the people on this occasion, Haggai capitalizes on the two themes of the Temple and the messianic fulfillment. He admits that the second Temple doesn't appear as glorious as the first (v.3), but it will still be the sign of God's covenant with Israel (vv.4-5). The external sign of the covenant is less imposing, but the Lord's promise is just as real and strong. The covenant is still as firm as it was at Sinai. "I am with you . . . . my spirit abides among you; fear not" (vv.4-5; RSV's capitalizing of "spirit" is an anachronism). Ultimately, when the Lord reveals his reign in Jerusalem completely, all treasures of the world will rightfully flow toward the holy mountain, and the new Temple will be even more imposing than that of Solomon (v.9).

The coming of the messianic kingdom is portrayed in the traditional terms of cosmic upheaval (vv.6, 21: Amos 8:8-9; Isa 13:13; Joel 2:10; 4:16). The Lord will shake the nations as a fruit harvester shaking trees. The Letter to the Hebrews uses this image from Haggai to emphasize that in Christ the foretold messianic kingdom has come, a kingdom that cannot be shaken like the worldly kingdoms: "Let us be grateful for receiving a kingdom that cannot be shaken, and thus let us offer to God acceptable worship, with reverence and awe; for our God is a consuming fire" (Heb 12:28-29). Haggai, however, is looking to the kingdom still in the future, and perceives that the conjunction of political turmoil in the Persian empire with the rebuilding of the Temple has messianic significance. He will focus its meaning on the governor of Judah in his final oracle.

I WILL SHAKE THE HEAVENS
2:10-23

[10]On the twenty-fourth day of the ninth month, in the second year of Darius, the word of the LORD came by

Haggai the prophet, "Thus says the LORD of hosts:
Ask the priests to decide this question, ¹²'If one carries
holy flesh in the skirt of his garment, and touches with
his skirt bread, or pottage, or wine, or oil, or any kind
of food, does it become holy?'" The priests answered,
"No." ¹³Then said Haggai, "If one who is unclean by
contact with a dead body touches any of these, does it
become unclean?" The priests answered, "It does become
unclean." ¹⁴Then Haggai said, "So is it with this people,
and with this nation before me, says the LORD; and so
with every work of their hands; and what they offer
there is unclean. ¹⁵Pray now, consider what will come
to pass from this day onward. Before a stone was placed
upon a stone in the temple of the LORD, ¹⁶how did you
fare? When one came to a heap of twenty measures,
there were but ten; when one came to the winevat to draw
fifty measures, there were but twenty. ¹⁷I smote you and
all the products of your toil with blight and mildew and
hail; yet you did not return to me, says the LORD.
¹⁸Consider from this day onward, from the twenty-
fourth day of the ninth month. Since the day that the
foundation of the LORD'S temple was laid, consider: ¹⁹Is
the seed yet in the barn? Do the vine, the fig tree, the
pomegranate, and the olive tree still yield nothing?
From this day on I will bless you."

²⁰The word of the LORD came a second time to
Haggai on the twenty-fourth day of the month, ²¹"Speak
to Zerubbabel, governor of Judah, saying, I am about
to shake the heavens and the earth, ²²and to overthrow
the throne of kingdoms; I am about to destroy the
strength of the kingdoms of the nations, and overthrow
the chariots and their riders; and the horses and their
riders shall go down, every one by the sword of his fellow.
²³On that day, says the LORD of hosts, I will take you,
O Zerubbabel my servant, the son of Shealtiel, says the
LORD, and make you like a signet ring; for I have chosen
you, says the LORD of hosts."

The concluding oracles, as mentioned already, are proclaimed exactly three months from the day the rebuilding began. The first involves an instruction by the priests on ritual cleanness and uncleanness (vv.12-14). The point of this curious debate seems to be that in Jewish law uncleanness is considered more contagious than holiness. The application may be that the contamination of some of the Jews through their exile in Babylon had affected all; or possibly this is part of the argument against permitting the Samaritans to help in the reconstruction (Ezra 4:3). Now that the people have returned to the Lord (indicated by their beginning the work on the Temple), they will no longer be considered unclean and the Lord will bless them (vv.17-19).

The Lord's promise to Zerubbabel may be read in a completely religious sense or with an admixture of political (revolutionary) meaning. Perhaps the ambiguity is intended to protect the principals against political reprisal. If Haggai envisioned political independence of Judah with Zerubbabel as a new David, he was certainly disappointed when Darius quelled the disturbances and consolidated his authority throughout the empire, including Judah. But the spiritual sense of the prophecy was there, too, and remained to continue to spur hopes among the Jews for generations to come. Whether or not Zerubbabel was to be a military leader like David, he was a king of David's line. The words describing his election (v.23) are traditional for an important role in salvation history: "I will take you" (Josh 24:3 = Abraham; 2 Sam 7:8 = David); "my servant" (Gen 26:24 = Abraham; 1 Kgs 11:13 = David). Yahweh will make him like a signet ring used for sealing official documents: Zerubbabel's rule has divine authority. With this promise Yahweh reverses the words addressed to Jehoiachin ("Coniah"), Zerubbabel's royal ancestor, as found in Jeremiah 22:24.

Bibliography

P. R. Ackroyd, *Exile and Restoration.* Pages 153-170.

J. G. Baldwin, *Haggai, Zechariah, Malachi,* (Tyndale OT. Commentaries) London: Tyndale Press, 1972.

F. M. Cross, "Reconstruction of the Judean Restoration," *JBL* 94 (March, 1975) 4-18.

G. Denzer, *The Books of Haggai, Zechariah, Malachi, Joel* (Old Testament Reading Guide, 21). Collegeville: Liturgical Press, 1966. Pages 3-10.

F. McDonagh, B. Robinson, and H. Swanston, *Prophets II* (Scripture Discussion Commentary, 4). London and Sydney: Sheed and Ward; Chicago; Acta Foundation, 1972. Pages 127-133.

R. Mason, *The Books of Haggai, Zechariah and Malachi* (Cambridge Bible Commentary). Cambridge and New York. Cambridge University Press, 1977.

Zechariah

ZECHARIAH

ZECHARIAH WAS ACTIVE in the same time and place as Haggai and dealt with the same issues—messianism, the rebuilding of the Temple, the rule of Yahweh through Zerubbabel—with some additions and different emphases. As with Haggai, we have practically no independent information about Zechariah, except that he seems to have been from a priestly family, and was possibly a Temple priest himself (see Neh 12:16). This would help to explain his interest in the priesthood and the Temple liturgy. Zechariah's oracles span a two-year period, beginning in October-November, 520 B.C. (two months after those of Haggai). His major utterance, a series of visions, took place three months later; there is a final oracle in November-December, 518 B.C.

Zechariah the prophet is responsible for only the first eight chapters of the book which bears his name. Chapters 9-14, which never mention Zechariah, are universally recognized to be a compilation of later material with different interests and in a different style. These chapters, often referred to as Second Zechariah, will be treated as a separate book in its chronological sequence after the Book of Joel.

FIRST ORACLE: RETURN TO ME
1:1-6

1 In the eighth month, in the second year of Darius, the word of the LORD came to Zechariah the son of Berechiah, son of Iddo, the prophet, saying, ²"The LORD was very angry with your fathers. ³Therefore say to them, Thus says the LORD of hosts: Return to me, says the LORD of hosts, and I will return to you, says the LORD of hosts. ⁴Be not like your fathers, to whom the former prophets cried out, 'Thus says the LORD of hosts, Return from your evil ways and from your evil deeds.' But they did not hear or heed me, says the LORD. ⁵Your fathers, where are they? And the prophets, do they live for ever? ⁶But my words and my statutes, which I commanded my servants the prophets, did they not overtake your fathers? So they repented and said, As the LORD of hosts purposed to deal with us for our ways and deeds, so has he dealt with us."

Zechariah begins his prophesying in October-November, 520 B.C., two months after the first discourse of Haggai. Zechariah is usually elsewhere identified only as the "son of Iddo" (Ezra 5:1; 6:14; Neh 12:16). The connection with Berechiah is probably a confusion with another Zechariah in Isaiah 8:2 through scribal error. Jesus refers to "the blood of Zechariah the son of Berachiah" (Mt 23:35), still another Zechariah, the son of Jehoiada, who was a prophet put to death by the order of King Joash of Judah in the ninth century B.C. Jesus' confusion of the two prophets is often pointed out as an example of the thoroughness of his incarnation, becoming human to the point of making factual errors in accepting what was probably a traditional reference of his times.

The destruction of Jerusalem is a punishment for the sins of the "fathers," not the ancients but Jeremiah's generation. Yahweh was "angry indeed" (v.2: NAB) with the

Hebrews, but not as angry ("very angry": v.15) as he is now with Babylon and Israel's other persecutors (a contrast in the Hebrew of verses 2 and 15 not clear in RSV). God made these nations his instruments for the correction of his people, an interpretation familiar among the prophets (Isa 10:5; Jer 25:9), but they went too far in their cruelty: ". . . while I was angry but a little they furthered the disaster" (v.15). In this way the prophet reiterates Yahweh's sovereignty even though outsiders take the defeat of his people as a sign of his weakness among the gods.

The call for a return to the Lord (vv.3-4) is a summons to conversion in the prophetic tradition: "Come, let us return to the Lord, for he has torn, that he may heal us" (Hos 6:1; see Amos 4:6, 8-9; Hos 2:9; Jer 3:22; 26:3). The quotation in verse 4 is from Jeremiah (25:5), a "former prophet": in the sense of "pre-exilic"; "former prophet" in a later time was applied to the historical books of Joshua, Judges, 1-2 Samuel, and 1-2 Kings, which told the story of early prophetic activity in Israel. The notion of total repentance or change of heart urged here is behind the New Testament Greek term for conversion, *metanoia*, as preached by John the Baptist, Jesus and the first Christian preachers (Mk 1:4-6, 15; Acts 2:38).

Those prophets are gone now but the word of the Lord lives on. The word of the Lord has an almost independent existence in Hebrew thought. A prophet is the steward of this word, not its master; thus he can speak only the word given to him (Num 23:18, 26). It is like a burning fire in his heart (Jer 20:9), or like a bird of prey released by the falconer (Isa 9:8), or like rain dropping on the parched earth (Isa 55:10-11). The word is powerful, trustworthy and effective, because it bears Yahweh's own authority. In the Old Testament, wisdom came to be personified and is said to have been with God before creation, to have been active at creation; just as God is said to have created the world through his word (Gen 1; Ps 33:6). This perception, in which wisdom and the word are brought together, will culminate in the vision of Jesus as the word or wisdom of God in the New Testament (Jn 1:1; 1 Cor 1:24; Heb 1:1-4). Here the word proclaimed by the prophets was not killed when they were; it lived on to "overtake" the rebellious (v.6; see 7:7). On the positive side, the covenant promise of the Lord lives on to produce a sure fulfillment (Hab 2:3).

FIRST VISION: THE FOUR HORSEMEN
1:7-17

⁷On the twenty-fourth day of the eleventh month which is the month of Shebat, in the second year of Darius, the word of the LORD came to Zechariah the son of Berechiah, son of Iddo, the prophet; and Zechariah said, ⁸"I saw in the night, and behold, a man riding upon a red horse! He was standing among the myrtle trees in the glen; and behind him were red, sorrel, and white horses. ⁹Then I said, 'What are these, my lord?' The angel who talked with me said to me, 'I will show you what they are.' ¹⁰So the man who was standing among the myrtle trees answered, 'These are they whom the LORD has sent to patrol the earth.' ¹¹And they answered the angel of the LORD who was standing among the myrtle trees, 'We have patrolled the earth, and behold, all the earth remains at rest.' ¹²Then the angel of the LORD said, 'O LORD of hosts, how long wilt thou have no mercy on Jerusalem and the cities of Judah, against which thou hast had indignation these seventy years?' ¹³And the LORD answered gracious and comforting words to the angel who talked with me. ¹⁴So the angel who talked with me said to me, 'Cry out, Thus says the LORD of hosts: I am exceedingly jealous for Jerusalem and for Zion. ¹⁵And I am very angry with the nations that are at ease; for while I was angry but a little they furthered the disaster. ¹⁶Therefore, thus says the LORD, I have returned to Jerusalem with compassion; my house shall be built in it, says the LORD of hosts,

and the measuring line shall be stretched out over Jerusalem. [17]Cry again, Thus says the LORD of hosts: My cities shall again overflow with prosperity, and the LORD will again comfort Zion and again choose Jerusalem.'"

The first oracle of Zechariah was very brief, a keynote, but the second oracle three months later (January-February, 519) is a long one, producing the bulk of the written material we have from this prophet (1:7 - 6:8). In a series of eight visions, Zechariah presents to his disillusioned people a message of hope for the future. His writing in this section is an early example of apocalyptic writing, a revelation or "unveiling" (from Greek *apocalypsis*) of things hidden. Apocalyptic writing is found in early form also in Ezekiel and in portions of Isaiah (Isa 24-28); later a more developed style appears in Zechariah 9-14, Daniel, and Revelation. Hallmarks of this literature are presentation of the message in dreams or visions, often through an angel, and exotic symbolism. The symbols are not so much visual as conceptual: each element of the vision has a meaning not to be lost when images are heaped one on top of another. The goal is not a grotesque visual image but a rich conceptual one. (Apocalyptic literature is treated of in greater detail by John J. Collins in volume 16 of this series.)

In the first vision four horsemen assigned to patrol the earth report on the situation of the Persian Empire. After the eruption of events surrounding the death of Cambyses II and the accession of Darius, the earth is at rest (v.11). But in contrast to this, Judah and her inhabitants are still suffering the consequences of the destruction and the Exile: they are not at peace (v.12). The angel speaks on behalf of the people, asking whether the seventy years of hardship prophesied by Jeremiah (Jer 25:11), now virtually complete (587 to 519 B.C.), is not enough punishment. The style of questioning here recalls the method of Ezekiel (Ezek

37:3); the response of Yahweh recalls the message of another prophet of the exile: "Speak tenderly to Jerusalem, and cry to her that her warfare is ended, that her iniquity is pardoned" (Isa 40:2). Instead of being "very angry" with Judah, as he is with her hostile neighbors, Yahweh is "exceedingly jealous" for her (v.14).

Earlier the Hebrews had been chided for complacency (Amos 6:1; Isa 32:9-11); now it is the other nations' turn (v.15). Because his people are returning to him, Yahweh will "return" to them and give them consolation and comfort.

SECOND VISION: THE HORNS AND THE BLACKSMITHS 1:18-21 (NAB: 2:1-4)

[18]And I lifted my eyes and saw, and behold, four horns! [19]And I said to the angel who talked with me, "What are these?" And he answered me, "These are the horns which have scattered Judah, Israel, and Jerusalem." [20]Then the LORD showed me four smiths. [21]And I said, "What are these coming to do?" He answered, "These are the horns which scattered Judah, so that no man raised his head; and these have come to terrify them, to cast down the horns of the nations who lifted up their horns against the land of Judah to scatter it."

Verses 18-21 of Chapter One in RSV (following the Greek and Latin versions) are verses 1-4 of Chapter Two in the Hebrew text and many modern versions (e.g. JB, NAB). This passage tells of the second vision of four horns and four blacksmiths, the "horns" representing the hostile powers of Babylon and other enemies who have harassed Judah. The blacksmiths are Yahweh's agents to punish those nations, probably by forging the weapons for their destruction.

THIRD VISION: MEASURING THE NEW CITY
2:1-13

2 And I lifted my eyes and saw, and behold, a man with a measuring line in his hand! ²Then I said, "Where are you going?" And he said to me, "To measure Jerusalem, to see what is its breadth and what is its length." ³And behold, the angel who talked with me came forward, and another angel came forward to meet him, ⁴and said to him, "Run, say to that young man, 'Jerusalem shall be inhabited as villages without walls, because of the multitude of men and cattle in it. ⁵For I will be to her a wall of fire round about, says the LORD, and I will be the glory within her.'"

⁶Ho! ho! Flee from the land of the north, says the LORD; for I have spread you abroad as the four winds of the heavens, says the LORD. ⁷Ho! Escape to Zion, you who dwell with the daughter of Babylon. ⁸For thus said the LORD of hosts, after his glory sent me to the nations who plundered you, for he who touches you touches the apple of his eye: ⁹"Behold, I will shake my hand over them, and they shall become plunder for those who served them. Then you will know that the LORD of hosts has sent me. ¹⁰Sing and rejoice, O daughter of Zion; for lo, I come and I will dwell in the midst of you, says the LORD. ¹¹And many nations shall join themselves to the LORD in that day, and shall be my people; and I will dwell in the midst of you, and you shall know that the LORD of hosts has sent me to you. ¹²And the LORD will inherit Judah as his portion in the holy land, and will again choose Jerusalem."

¹³Be silent, all flesh, before the LORD; for he has roused himself from his holy dwelling.

Zechariah's third vision begins with the image of a man (or an angel) measuring the dimensions of the new Jerusalem. This image, already alluded to in Chapter One (v.16), is expanded from Ezekiel's vision of the measurement of the new Temple (Ezek 40:3; 41:13) and will reappear in the Book of Revelation (11:1). This chapter alerts us more than the first to the continuity of imagery and themes in Zechariah with that of Ezekiel and that other exilic prophet, Second Isaiah (Isa 40-55). And as with the measuring line, many of these elements are taken up much later by the author of Revelation.

Startling news comes to the surveyor; it's useless to plan walls for Jerusalem, because her population in the future is going to be so great that people will cover her like a flood (v.4). The Lord himself will be a "wall of fire" around her, and "the glory within her" (v.5). This is the theme of messianic universalism forged in the Exile (Isa 54:1-3; 56:6-8); it is stated even more clearly later in the chapter (vv.10-11). Possibly there is also a subliminal warning: any attempt to restore the walls at this time will be seen as a treasonable thrust by Persian authorities; this was one of the criticisms that would afflict Nehemiah (Neh 1:6). The wall of fire is a way of applying the nomadic cloud of fire in the desert (Ex 13:21-22; Num 9:15-23) to the settled life of the city dweller. God will remain with his people as their protector. The return of the glory of the Lord to Jerusalem was envisioned in Ezekiel (43:1-3). Revelation sees the fulfillment in Christ in the heavenly Jerusalem: "The city has no need of sun or moon to shine upon it, for the glory of God is its light, and its lamp is the Lamb" (Rev 21:22).

The "Ho! ho!" of verse 6 is a call to attention ("Up! Up!" in NAB) for the exiles remaining in the land of the north, Babylon. They are in danger because the Lord is coming to punish their captors, and innocent people may get caught in the fallout. They must hurry to participate in the glorious revival of Jerusalem. The Lord will "shake his hand" over them in a menacing gesture (v.9; see Isa 11:15; 19:16) while he protects his people from further harm at their hands. The tables will be turned on the Babylonians; their slaves will plunder them.

In terms very reminiscent of the oracle of Zephaniah, the prophet suddenly changes his tone from recrimination and concern about protection to a cry of resounding joy: "Sing and rejoice, O daughter of Zion!" (v.10; see Zeph 3:14-15). The reason for joy is the presence of the Lord in the midst of his people, the permanent fulfillment of the age-old promise of God to his elect: "I will be with you" (see Hag 1:13). This same connection of rejoicing, freedom from fear, and presence of the Lord comes to the fore in the annunciation to Mary: "Hail, O favored one, the Lord is with you! . . . Do not be afraid" (Lk 1:28, 30). Verses 10-13 are a further reflection on the vision of the measuring line in verses 1-5; as verses 6-9 complement the vision of the horns and blacksmiths in 1:18-21.

In the age that is coming, even the foreign nations will "be my people" (v.11). This goes beyond Haggai, who sees the people coming to Jerusalem only to deposit their treasures (Hag 2:10-14). Covenant language seals the promise for Jerusalem: "inherit," "portion," "choose." Here for the first time Judah is called the "holy land" (v.12; Wis 12:3; 2 Macc 1:7). The proper attitude before the Lord as he begins to bring his promise to fulfillment is silence (v.13), a silence not of fear, but of faith and confidence (Hab 2:20; Isa 41:1).

FOURTH VISION: JOSHUA THE HIGH PRIEST
3:1-7

3 Then he showed me Joshua the high priest standing before the angel of the LORD, and Satan standing at his right hand to accuse him. ²And the LORD said to Satan, "The LORD rebuke you, O Satan! The LORD who has chosen Jerusalem rebuke you! Is not this a brand plucked from the fire?" ³Now Joshua was standing before the angel, clothed with filthy garments. ⁴And the angel said to those who were standing before him, "Remove the

filthy garments from him." And to him he said, "Behold,
I have taken your iniquity away from you, and I will
clothe you with rich apparel." ⁵And I said, "Let them put
a clean turban on his head." So they put a clean turban
on his head and clothed him with garments; and the angel
of the LORD was standing by.

⁶And the angel of the LORD enjoined Joshua, ⁷"Thus
says the LORD of hosts: If you will walk in my ways and
keep my charge, then you shall rule my house and have
charge of my courts, and I will give you the right of
access among those who are standing here."

The fourth vision introduces the spiritual leader of the
returned exiles, Joshua the high priest. Joshua stands for
both the post-exilic remnant and for the priesthood of the
second Temple. As such he takes his place before the
heavenly court to be accused of the uncleanness that attaches
to the people from their time of foreign exile. Satan (or
"the accuser") in this vision as in the book of Job (Job
1:6-12) is one of the heavenly court, an agent of God in
punishing humans for their sinfulness. Only later will
Scripture speak of Satan as hostile to God as well as man
(Wis 2:24). An advance in angelology surfaces here. Before
the exile, God was the agent of evil as the means of punishing sin; afterward, demons are his intermediaries for
correction of human evil. The difference is evident in two
accounts of David's (evil) plan to take a census, one pre-
exilic (2 Sam 24:1), the other post-exilic (1 Chr 21:1).
This time, however, Satan is halted in his accusations.
Jerusalem has had enough punishment and the time has
come for restoration. "The Lord who has chosen Jerusalem
rebuke you!" (v.2). The description of "a brand plucked
from the fire" is a proverbial way of speaking of a close
escape, already applied to Israel by the prophet Amos
(Amos 4:11). Here the reference is to Joshua as the representative of Jerusalem and the whole people rescued from
the Exile. His filthy garments represent the uncleanness

because of contamination in a foreign land, and perhaps the guilt of the pre-exilic community which led to the Exile, and which still pertains to the remnant historically continuous with the forefathers.

Joshua is refurbished with clean garments and with a clean turban (v.5). The turban, as well as the inscription engraved on it, are a renewal of the pertinent vestments of Aaron designed for the inauguration of his ministry as high priest (Ex 28:36-38). Aaron's turban was associated with purification of the people's guilt; the inscription reads "Holy is the Lord." Then, in the name of the priests, Joshua is given rule over the Temple, a greater role than in the days of the kings, and a special right of access. The author of the Letter to the Hebrews sees Jesus fulfilling these roles for the new people of God as the high priest par excellence, one who can "make expiation for the sins of the people" (Heb 2:17) and who has "passed through the heavens" to become the means of access to God himself: "Let us then with confidence draw near to the throne of grace" (4:14,16).

THE BRANCH
3:8-10

> 8Hear now, O Joshua the high priest, you and your friends who sit before you, for they are men of good omen: behold, I will bring my servant the Branch. 9For behold, upon the stone which I have set before Joshua, upon a single stone with seven facets, I will engrave its inscription, says the LORD of hosts, and I will remove the guilt of this land in a single day. 10In that day, says the LORD of hosts, every one of you will invite his neighbor under his vine and under his fig tree."

The priests are "men of good omen" (v.8) because the restoration of the priesthood is a sign of the messianic age. With this will come the "Branch," the messianic figure who will keep the David dynasty and hopes alive (Isa 11:1; Jer 23:5; Ezek 17:22). Here the reference is to Zerubbabel, the governor of the restored Jerusalem, who is also referred to as "my servant" by Haggai (Hag 2:23). "Branch" was translated by the Greek Old Testament as *anatolē*, the "rising" (of the sun), which then became a messianic title applied to Jesus in the canticle of the New Testament Zechariah, father of John the Baptist: "He, the Dayspring (*anatolē*), shall visit us in his mercy" (Lk 1:78 NAB).

The "stone" of verse 9 has been a puzzle to commentators. It is either to be associated with the engraving on Aaron's turban (Ex 28:36; see Zech 3:5) or with the engraving of the stones on his breastplate (Ex 28:9-14), or is to be considered a symbol for the Temple (Isa 28:16). The seven facets are interpreted in Zechariah 4:10 as the eyes of the Lord, symbolizing Yahweh's presence and all-pervasive knowledge. On the messianic "day," all the guilt of Israel will be removed; the prosperity of the "vine and fig tree" will be the same as in the time of Solomon, the builder of the first Temple (v.11; 1 Kgs 4:25).

FIFTH VISION: THE LAMPSTAND
4:1-14

4 And the angel who talked with me came again, and waked me, like a man that is wakened out of his sleep. ²And he said to me, "What do you see?" I said, "I see, and behold, a lampstand all of gold, with a bowl on the top of it, and seven lamps on it, with seven lips on each of the lamps which are on the top of it. ³And there are two olive trees by it, one on the right of the bowl and the other on its left." ⁴And I said to the angel who talked with me, "What are these, my lord?" ⁵Then the angel who talked with me answered me, "Do you not know what these are?" I said, "No, my lord." ⁶Then he said to me, "This is the word of the LORD to Zerubbabel: Not by might, nor by power, but by my Spirit, says the LORD of hosts.

[7]What are you, O great mountain? Before Zerubbabel you shall become a plain; and he shall bring forward the top stone amid shouts of 'Grace, grace to it!'" [8]Moreover the word of the LORD came to me, saying, [9]"The hands of Zerubbabel have laid the foundation of this house; his hands shall also complete it. Then you will know that the LORD of hosts has sent me to you. [10]For whoever has despised the day of small things shall rejoice, and shall see the plummet in the hand of Zerubbabel.
"These seven are the eyes of the LORD, which range through the whole earth." [11]Then I said to him, "What are these two olive trees on the right and the left of the lampstand?" [12]And a second time I said to him, "What are these two branches of the olive trees, which are beside the two golden pipes from which the oil is poured out?" [13]He said to me, "Do you not know what these are?" I said, "No, my lord." [14]Then he said, "These are the two anointed who stand by the Lord of the whole earth."

The lampstand, bowl and lamps comprise a complicated symbolism for God and the agents of his activity. The focus of attention is not on this image but on the identity of the two olive trees (v.3). In the final verse the answer to the question of verse 4 is revealed: "These are the two anointed who stand by the Lord of the whole earth" (v.14). In other words, the two olive trees are Zerubbabel the political leader and Joshua the religious leader. They are the source of the oil that lights God's lamps; apparently this means they are his chosen agents of princely and priestly power. They are literally called the two "messiahs" (v.14), a statement that gave rise in Israel to the tradition of two coming messiahs, a messiah of David and a messiah of Levi or Aaron, which is mentioned in apocryphal literature and affected the expectation of the Qumran community which produced the Dead Sea Scrolls.

Zerubbabel receives special attention in the vision. The verses addressed to him are probably out of place in the context, but their import is clear. Zerubbabel is to rely on divine power, not military might. Yahweh will see to it that the Temple is restored and that Zerubbabel is able to place the capstone himself. The "great mountain"(v.7) may mean the many obstacles and difficulties (Isa 40:3-4) that have so far hampered plans of rebuilding. Zechariah, like Haggai, has heard the criticisms of those who compare the meager beginnings of the new Temple with the grandeur of the Temple of Solomon (Hag 2:3). But the Lord brings encouragement: "Whoever has despised the day of small things shall rejoice" (v.10). A thousand miles begins with a single step; often God's acts of salvation begin insignificantly, as in the vision of an old shepherd (Ex 3:1-3) or in a word to an obscure maiden in Galilee (Lk 1:26-33), and depend on the faith of God's instruments to be carried out.

SIXTH VISION: THE FLYING SCROLL
5:1-4

> 5 Again I lifted my eyes and saw, and behold, a flying scroll! ²And he said to me, "What do you see?" I answered, "I see a flying scroll; its length is twenty cubits, and its breadth ten cubits." ³Then he said to me, "This is the curse that goes out over the face of the whole land; for every one who steals shall be cut off henceforth according to it, and every one who swears falsely shall be cut off henceforth according to it. ⁴I will send it forth, says the LORD of hosts, and it shall enter the house of the thief, and the house of him who swears falsely by my name; and it shall abide in his house and consume it, both timber and stones."

The two visions in Chapter Five portray symbolically the cleansing from sinfulness that must precede the inauguration of the messianic kingdom. Thus these visions parallel the replacement of Joshua's filthy garments by clean robes in the fourth vision (3:1-5). Vision Six presents an enormous flying scroll, thirty feet by fifteen feet, with curses for thieves and perjurers. These dimensions are the exact measurements of the porch of Solomon's Temple (1 Kgs 6:3). The entrance to the new Temple is blocked until guilt is wiped away. Sinfulness must be cast out. The sins mentioned are inclusive of all sin, those against God, "swearing falsely by my name" (perjury), and those against people (stealing).

These curses are not a random feature of the renewal of worship in the Temple. The covenant formula by which God took the people of Israel for his own contained curses that would fall on those who broke the covenant (Dt 28:15-19). The renewal of the covenant at the time of the inauguration of new life in the city or worship in the new Temple would involve a reading of the Law, with the terms of the covenant, the promises and the curses. The curse is sent "to the house" of the thief or perjurer, who must bear individual responsibility for the crime. The curse will "abide in his house and consume it" (v.4). Here again as in 1:6 we encounter the power of a word to carry out its purpose almost as a living person. Worth reading in this connection is the procedure for determining the guilt or innocence of a woman accused of adultery detailed in the Book of Numbers (5:11-28). The curse is "washed off" the scroll and drunk by the accused; it will search her entrails and make the decision. This notion of the word gives an idea of the depth and power the concept of a "word of God" could have for the Hebrew people, though admittedly the magical element must be filtered out in order to understand God's message as an authentic "word of faith" (Rom 10:8).

SEVENTH VISION: THE FLYING BARREL
5:5-11

⁵Then the angel who talked with me came forward and said to me, "Lift your eyes, and see what this is that

goes forth." ⁶And I said, "What is it?" He said, "This is the ephah that goes forth." And he said, "This is their iniquity in all the land." ⁷And behold, the leaden cover was lifted, and there was a woman sitting in the ephah! ⁸And he said, "This is Wickedness." And he thrust her back into the ephah, and thrust down the leaden weight upon its mouth. ⁹Then I lifted my eyes and saw, and behold, two women coming forward! The wind was in their wings; they had wings like the wings of a stork, and they lifted up the ephah between earth and heaven. ¹⁰Then I said to the angel who talked with me. "Where are they taking the ephah?" ¹¹He said to me, "To the land of Shinar, to build a house for it; and when this is prepared, they will set the ephah down there on its base."

The next vision presents the same idea of purification of the land from sin before the messianic era comes in fullness. The ephah is a container for about a bushel of grain. The New English Bible's "barrel" makes the vision more comprehensible. The barrel contains all the wickedness of Israel, personified by a woman either because the word "wickedness" is feminine in Hebrew, or because Israel's fundamental sin, falling for gods of other nations by syncretism and idolatry, has been termed "adultery" or "harlotry" by the prophets (Jer 3:8; Hos 1:2). This latter reason seems strong in the light of Ezekiel's influence on Zechariah: Ezekiel draws a vivid picture of Israel as a wayward woman (Ezek 16).

To balance the negative image of the Wickedness of Israel portrayed as a woman, it is two women who take this sinfulness from the land so that it may truly be "holy" (2:12). They have wings like a stork because they must make a long flight to the North. Their destination is the "land of Shinar," an ancient name for the region of Babylon (Gen 10:10; 11:2; Dan 1:2). There a temple will be built for Wickedness in the symbolic center of the pagan world. The contrast is harsh: in Jerusalem, once defeated by Babylon, a Temple is being constructed for the worship of the true God; but Babylon is reduced to worshiping sin, and not just any sin, but the sin cast off by Jerusalem.

EIGHTH VISION: THE FOUR CHARIOTS
6:1-8

6 And again I lifted my eyes and saw, and behold, four chariots came out from between two mountains; and the mountains were mountains of bronze. ²The first chariot had red horses, the second black horses, ³the third white horses, and the fourth chariot dappled gray horses. ⁴Then I said to the angel who talked with me, "What are these, my lord?" ⁵And the angel answered me, "These are going forth to the four winds of heaven, after presenting themselves before the Lord of all the earth. ⁶The chariot with the black horses goes toward the north country, the white ones go toward the west country, and the dappled ones go toward the south country." ⁷When the steeds came out, they were impatient to get off and patrol the earth. And he said, "Go, patrol the earth." So they patrolled the earth. ⁸Then he cried to me, "Behold, those who go toward the north country have set my Spirit at rest in the north country."

The vision of the chariots is in many ways a doublet of the vision of the four horsemen (1:8-17). Again these are agents of the Lord sent as scouts to the four corners of the earth. The "four winds" (v.5) emphasize the universal dominion of Yahweh. The mention of the two mountains is ironically a reference to Babylonian mythology, where the entrance to the realm of the sun-god Shamash is marked by two great columns. The mission of the fourth chariot (to the east) has dropped out of the text in its transmission. But the most important direction is, as usual in these visions, to the north, the direction of Babylon. Earlier, the nations were found to be "at rest" (1:11,15); here the

Lord's spirit is at rest: either, in one sense, that the exiles
have been roused to return and build the Temple, or
in another, that the Lord's anger against Babylon is
satisfied.

A CROWN FOR THE BRANCH
6:9-15

⁹And the word of the LORD came to me: ¹⁰"Take
from the exiles Heldai, Tobijah, and Jedaiah, who have
arrived from Babylon; and go the same day to the house
of Josiah, the son of Zephaniah. ¹¹Take from them silver
and gold, and make a crown, and set it upon the head
of Joshua, the son of Jehozadak, the high priest; ¹²and
say to him, 'Thus says the LORD of hosts, "Behold, the
man whose name is the Branch: for he shall grow up in
his place, and he shall build the temple of the LORD.
¹³It is he who shall build the temple of the LORD, and
shall bear royal honor, and shall sit and rule upon his
throne. And there shall be a priest by his throne, and
peaceful understanding shall be between them both.'"
¹⁴And the crown shall be in the temple of the LORD as a
reminder to Heldai, Tobijah, Jedaiah, and Josiah the
son of Zephaniah.
¹⁵"And those who are far off shall come and help to
build the temple of the LORD; and you shall know that
the LORD of hosts has sent me to you. And this shall
come to pass, if you will diligently obey the voice of the
LORD your God."

The eighth vision is followed by a sort of historical
appendix in which instructions are given for the coronation
(probably meant symbolically) of the new king of Israel
as a messianic figure. This section is an excellent example
of the "doctoring" a text may receive when circumstances
change after it has been written. As it stands, the passage
describes the coronation of Joshua, named the "Branch,"

identified as the builder of the Temple, seated on the throne of Jerusalem. There is virtually unanimous agreement among scholars that the name in verse 11 has been changed from Zerubbabel to Joshua. Zerubbabel is elsewhere identified as the Temple builder (4:9) and Joshua is elsewhere distinct from the Branch (3:8) as the priest is separate from the Branch in 6:14.

Why was Zerubbabel's name removed from this coronation scene and replaced by the name of the high priest? History did not turn out in every detail as Haggai and Zechariah had hoped. They had hung their hopes on Zerubbabel as the Davidic ruler who would be the first in a new line of powerful kings ruling in Jerusalem until the arrival of the definitive messianic age. We do not know what happened to Zerubbabel. He is mentioned no more in the biblical or other literature. The speculation is that word reached Darius of an impending revolt in Jerusalem and Zerubbabel was removed. Apparently the kingship ended with him, for we are not aware of a successor. The leadership of the Jewish people after this time fell completely to the priests. The final editing of this passage took place when the high priest was the sole authority in Jerusalem. Since the hope of a Davidic revival had died, the present text was redirected toward the new set of circumstances.

To a modern reader this might seem a notorious example of "tampering with the text." It would be a serious breach for someone brought up according to our standards of historical writing. But the biblical compiler/editor sees his role as one of helping his co-religionists understand God's dealings with Israel. He is not simply responsible for reproducing the bare facts; sometimes the facts may need embellishment to bring out their true meaning. Prophetic writing has to be brought up to date to speak to new situations; visions that have become meaningless with the passage of time must be newly interpreted for the present generation.

The persons mentioned in verses 10 and 14 as "arrived from Babylon" have not been identified. Perhaps there was an undercurrent of dissent among the newly-returned about the leadership of the restored people. They may have had misgivings about the legitimacy of Zerubbabel (appointee of Babylon) as the Davidic ruler, or about the authority of the priests, which would now be greater than at any time before the Exile. This chapter might originally have envisioned the crowning of both Joshua and Zerubbabel. The Hebrew text has the plural "crowns" in verses 11 and 14. The king and the priest are seated side by side in "peaceful understanding" (v.13). This vision would be an answer to the critics from Babylon.

The closing verse refers to the need of obedience in bringing the Lord's promises to fulfillment. This mention of obedience and its blessings is a balance to the message about sin and its curses in the preceding chapter. In Moses' covenant declaration, the list of curses is followed by an enumeration of blessings (Deut 28:1-14).

A QUESTION OF FASTING
7:1-7

7 In the fourth year of King Darius, the word of the LORD came to Zechariah on the fourth day of the ninth month, which is Chislev. ²Now the people of Bethel had sent Sharezer and Regem-melech and their men, to entreat the favor of the LORD, ³and to ask the priests of the house of the LORD of hosts and the prophets, "Should I mourn and fast in the fifth month, as I have done for so many years?" ⁴Then the word of the LORD of hosts came to me: ⁵"Say to all the people of the land and the priests, When you fasted and mourned in the fifth month and in the seventh, for these seventy years, was it for me that you fasted? ⁶And when you eat and when you drink, do you not eat for yourselves and drink for yourselves? ⁷When Jerusalem was inhabited and in prosperity, with her cities round about her, and the South and the lowland were inhabited, were not these the words which the LORD proclaimed by the former prophets?"

The narrative jumps two years to another oracle delivered about halfway through the construction of the Temple (November-December, 518). A delegation comes to ask the priests whether the fasts observed in commemoration of the fall of Jerusalem continue to be in effect now that the Exile is over and the Temple is nearly constructed. The inquiry concerns the fast of the fifth month, Ab (July-August), which had been held annually as a sign of mourning in remembrance of the fall of Jerusalem in 587 B.C. This observance later became known as the Ninth of Ab, an occasion for the liturgical reading of Lamentations, when the fall of Jerusalem to the Romans in 70 A.D. was the focus of the commemoration.

The answer to the question mentions another fast, that of the seventh month, Marheshwan (September-October), which mourned Gedaliah, the Jewish governor who had been assassinated shortly after his installation by the Babylonians following their takeover in Jerusalem (2 Kgs 25:22-26). The rest of the answer (in Chapter Eight) will mention two other fasts (see 8:19). Included with the response is a challenge in the language of the pre-exilic prophets: "Was it for me that you fasted?" (v.5). The religious observances cover up immorality. "On your fast day you carry out your own pursuits" (Isa 58:3).

TRUE ASCETICISM
7:8-14

> ⁸And the word of the LORD came to Zechariah, saying, ⁹"Thus says the LORD of hosts, Render true judgments, show kindness and mercy each to his brother, ¹⁰do not oppress the widow, the fatherless, the sojourner, or the poor; and let none of you devise evil against his brother in your heart." ¹¹But they refused to hearken, and turned a stubborn shoulder, and stopped their ears that they might not hear. ¹²They made their hearts like adamant lest they should hear the law and the words which the LORD of hosts had sent by his Spirit through

the former prophets. Therefore great wrath came from the LORD of hosts. [13]"As I called, and they would not hear, so they called, and I would not hear," says the LORD of hosts, [14]"and I scattered them with a whirlwind among all the nations which they had not known. Thus the land they left was desolate, so that no one went to and fro, and the pleasant land was made desolate."

The true renewal of life in Jerusalem in preparation for the advent of the messianic era means a change of heart that will express itself especially in social justice: honest judgments, kindness, mercy, care for the helpless. In an admonition characteristic of the Sermon on the Mount, the prophet warns against interior hostility (v.10: Mt 5:22).

It quickly becomes evident that this response to the question of fasting is just another opportunity to warn against the sins of the fathers. The people are compared to a stubborn child, turning away, fingers in ears (v.11). The sad irony is that the Lord was offering good things to his people, "the law and the words . . . sent by his spirit" (v.12). They turned down these good things and received wrath instead. Israel is termed the pleasant or desirable land; it became desolate (v.14). Yahweh is the Hound of Heaven, chasing his people to give them good things, but they (and we) are suspicious of his goodness and prefer to seek independent paths.

THE MESSIANIC AGE
8:1-8

8 And the word of the LORD of hosts came to me, saying, [2]"Thus says the LORD of hosts: I am jealous for Zion with great jealousy, and I am jealous for her with great wrath. [3]Thus says the LORD: I will return to Zion, and will dwell in the midst of Jerusalem, and Jerusalem shall be called the faithful city, and the mountain of the LORD of hosts, the holy mountain. [4]Thus says the

LORD of hosts: Old men and old women shall again sit in the streets of Jerusalem, each with staff in hand for very age. ⁵And the streets of the city shall be full of boys and girls playing in its streets. ⁶Thus says the LORD of hosts: If it is marvelous in the sight of the remnant of this people in these days, should it also be marvelous in my sight, says the LORD of hosts? ⁷Thus says the LORD of hosts: Behold, I will save my people from the east country and from the west country; ⁸and I will bring them to dwell in the midst of Jerusalem; and they shall be my people and I will be their God, in faithfulness and in righteousness."

This concluding chapter of the book has a loose connection with the preceding chapter (the question of fasting is taken up for a positive answer to balance the earlier negative one), but it has obviously undergone a lot of editing. It seems to be made up of ten separate oracles given on different occasions. The tone of the chapter is consistently hopeful and positive, which makes the book end on a reassuring note. It is full of messianic promises about the holy city. Just as Yahweh was faithful to his warnings in causing Jerusalem to suffer, so he is faithful to his promises of restoration. He is "jealous with great jealousy" for Zion (v.2; see 1:14).

Yahweh promises to "dwell" in the midst of Jerusalem (v.3). The verb used to express God's settling down with his people is rich with biblical memories. It is the Hebrew *shakan*, the word used to express God's presence with his people in a tent in early nomadic days (Ex 25:8; 29:46). Now it has the sense of messianic completion and finality. Christian believers recognize even this as a stage on the way. God's definitive dwelling with his people has taken place in Jesus Christ. John's Gospel makes this specific in saying: "The word became flesh and dwelt among us" (Jn 1:14). The word he uses is a form of *skenoun*, the Greek equivalent of *shakan*: "He pitched his tent among us." The Lord's presence will make Jerusalem truly the faithful city and Zion the holy mountain in the fulfillment of messianic titles.

The peace and prosperity envisioned for the whole society is dramatized in the calm retirement of the old and the unmolested play of the young (vv.4-5). Lamentations showed the disruption of the whole society in the suffering of the elders and the maidens (Lam 2:10). Though this turn of events seems impossible to the remnant of the Hebrews, it is not difficult for the Lord, who has demonstrated that his power and authority transcend national boundaries. He reaches beyond Israel to bring his people back from Babylon and Egypt, the east country and the west country (v.7). The remnant will be made to dwell (*shakan*) in the midst of Jerusalem with their God. The traditional promise is repeated: "They shall be my people and I will be their God" (v.8; Lev 26:12; Hos 2:21-25).

LET YOUR HANDS BE STRONG
8:9-13

> [9]Thus says the LORD of hosts: "Let your hands be strong, you who in these days have been hearing these words from the mouth of the prophets, since the day that the foundation of the house of the LORD of hosts was laid, that the temple might be built. [10]For before those days there was no wage for man or any wage for beast, neither was there any safety from the foe for him who went out or came in; for I set every man against his fellow. [11]But now I will not deal with the remnant of this people as in the former days, says the LORD of hosts. [12]For there shall be a sowing of peace; the vine shall yield its fruit, and the ground shall give its increase, and the heavens shall give their dew; and I will cause the remnant of this people to possess all these things. [13]And as you have been a byword of cursing among

the nations, O house of Judah and house of Israel, so will I save you and you shall be a blessing. Fear not, but let your hands be strong."

The oracle in these verses reintroduces the theme of the rebuilding of the Temple: this will be a major sign of the blessing of the Lord. Before this time fear and poverty reigned; now "Let your hands be strong" because all that is changing. This phrase serves as a theme-frame for the oracle (vv.9,13). In beautiful imagery the prophet tells of a renewal of the "covenant with the earth" made during the days of Noah (Gen 9:8-17): "There shall be a sowing of peace (*shalom*)" (v.12). Peace is not only the absence of conflict, as in Tacitus' damning comment about the Romans: "They make a desert and call it peace." Peace is the establishment of right order: the vine will yield fruit, the earth crops, the heavens dew (v.12). This peace is accompanied by prosperity. The right order among people will mean justice.

LOVE TRUTH AND PEACE
8:14-19

14For thus says the LORD of hosts: "As I purposed to do evil to you, when your fathers provoked me to wrath, and I did not relent, says the LORD of hosts, 15so again have I purposed in these days to do good to Jerusalem and to the house of Judah; fear not. 16These are the things that you shall do: Speak the truth to one another, render in your gates judgments that are true and make for peace, 17do not devise evil in your hearts against one another, and love no false oath, for all these things I hate, says the LORD."

18And the word of the LORD of hosts came to me, saying, 19"Thus says the LORD of hosts: The fast of the fourth month, and the fast of the fifth, and the fast of the seventh, and the fast of the tenth, shall be to the house of Judah seasons of joy and gladness, and cheerful feasts; therefore love truth and peace.

The nature of true peace as right relationship among people is indicated in the next oracle (vv.14-17), where the moral renewal necessary for the inauguration of the messianic era is to the center again: truth, justice, love, peace. Finally in verses 18 and 19 comes the thorough answer to the question about fasting in the time after the Exile. The fasts shall be turned into feasts (v.19); no more need for mourning. Besides the fasts mentioned in Chapter Seven, those of the fifth and seventh months, two other dates are mentioned, the fourth and the tenth months. The feast of the fourth month, Tammuz (June-July), recalled Babylon's first breach of Jerusalem's walls in the summer of 587 B.C. The feast of the tenth month, Tebet (December-January), remembered the beginning of the siege of Jerusalem in the preceding winter.

THE CENTER OF THE WORLD
8:20-23

> [20]"Thus says the LORD of hosts: Peoples shall yet come, even the inhabitants of many cities; [21]the inhabitants of one city shall go to another, saying, 'Let us go at once to entreat the favor of the LORD, and to seek the LORD of hosts; I am going.' [22]Many peoples and strong nations shall come to seek the LORD of hosts in Jerusalem, and to entreat the favor of the LORD. [23]Thus says the LORD of hosts: In those days ten men from the nations of every tongue shall take hold of the robe of a Jew, saying, 'Let us go with you, for we have heard that God is with you.'"

This collection of oracles ends the Book of Zechariah on a note of optimistic universalism. A few years before,

Israel was a subjugated nation in exile; its religion was ridiculed because of the apparent weakness of its God. Now all of that is reversed in the vision of the prophet. All peoples, even the "strong nations" (v.22), will recognize that Yahweh is the true God. Instead of ridiculing Jerusalem they will come hat in hand to entreat the favor of her Lord. They will ask help from each Jew, for "We have heard that God is with you" (v.23). This is an echo of the Immanuel prophecy (Isa 7:14), which in turn is based on the promise given to God's people throughout salvation history (Ex 3:12; Jer 1:8; Hag 2:4). Jesus will emphasize the divine choice of Israel: "Salvation is from the Jews" (Jn 4:22).

Bibliography

P. R. Ackroyd, *Exile and Restoration*, pages 171-217.

J. G. Baldwin, *Haggai, Zechariah, Malachi*, pages 58-208.

M. Barker, "The Two Figures in Zechariah," *HeyJ* 19 (January, 1978) 12-27.

G. Denzer, *The Books of Haggai, Zechariah, Malachi, Joel*, pages 11-24.

P. D. Hanson, *The Dawn of Apocalyptic*, Philadelphia: Fortress, 1975.

F. McDonagh, B. Robinson, and H. Swanston, *Prophets II*, pages 134-142.

D. Petersen, "Zerubbabel and the Jerusalem Temple Reconstruction," *CBQ* 36 (July, 1974), 366-372.

Malachi

MALACHI

Background

THE COMMENTARY ON MALACHI is placed after Zechariah 1-8, which it follows chronologically in the series of post-exilic books contained in the present collection. As explained above, Zechariah 9-14 will be treated under the title Second Zechariah after the Book of Joel, where these chapters fit chronologically. The reasons for this arrangement will be given in the introduction to Second Zechariah.

The prophecy of Malachi should be dated to the middle of the fifth century, or around 460—450 B.C., a little more than half a century after the triumphal completion of the new Temple. The prophet's identity is unknown. His name is given as "my messenger" or "Malachi" in the introductory verse (Mal 1:1) added by the editor; the editor took it from the mention of the sending of the messenger in Malachi 3:1. Though Zechariah 9-14 has intervened in the chronological sequence, the Book of Malachi has always been attached to these chapters in the Hebrew Bible. How did this happen? For some time, the most attractive theory has been the following: At the end of the collection of eleven shorter books of prophecy (Minor Prophets: Hosea, Joel, Amos, Obadiah, Jonah, Micah, Nahum, Habakkuk, Zephaniah, Haggai, Zechariah [1-8]) were three collections of prophecies, each introduced by the title, "An Oracle."

None of the three had the name of any prophet connected to it. In order to make the collection of minor prophets add up to the biblically significant number twelve, two of these collections were connected to the eleventh book of the series (Zechariah 1-8) and became Zechariah 9-11 and Zechariah 12-14. The third collection was made to stand as the separate book of Malachi.

That is as far as the relation of Malachi to Second Zechariah goes, however. The chapters attributed to Malachi belong to an earlier period and react to a different situation in Israel. Malachi reflects the next stage in the religious history of Israel after the time of the prophets Haggai and Zechariah. Haggai and Zechariah were concerned with the resettlement of the people returned from exile in Babylon and above all with the rebuilding of the Temple. This project was successfully completed in 515 B.C. Enthusiasm for Temple worship remained high for some time after this but by a natural process of erosion, the religious fervor aroused by the Second Temple began to wane. The books of Ezra and Nehemiah recount the sad state of affairs in Jerusalem in the second half of the fifth century B.C. which occasioned the mission of Nehemiah in 445 B.C. and the followup ministry of Ezra. (Their work will be discussed in a supplementary essay following the commentary on Malachi). Malachi describes the same sorry situation a few years before the arrival of Nehemiah.

Temple Abuses

The prophet lays great stress on the abuses that are ruining Temple worship. He condemns the priests, who have become the political as well as the religious leaders of the nation, for abuses in liturgy, for intermarriage with foreigners, for the spread of social injustices. Haggai and Zechariah had needed to arouse the people from their complacency fifty years after the Exile so that they would build the Temple; Malachi must shake them from their lassitude fifty years after the Temple construction.

This book's most memorable contribution to the New Testament is the image of the messenger sent to prepare the way to the Temple for Yahweh (3:1-3); this was applied to the precursor of the Lord in the Gospels (Mk 1:2; Mt 11:10). Malachi's vision of the pure universal offering (1:11) which will replace the flawed sacrifices in the messianic age may be alluded to in Jesus' description of worship "in spirit and truth" (Jn 4:23); it was interpreted by the Council of Trent as being fulfilled in the Eucharist.

The prophet employs a distinctive dialogue technique in challenging his contemporaries: an affirmation by the Lord or the prophet, a question or complaint by the listeners, then the prophet's (often harsh) response. This method was used to involve the readers more intimately and challenge them more personally.

FIRST WORD: YAHWEH'S FAITHFUL LOVE
1:1-5

1 The oracle of the word of the LORD to Israel by Malachi.
²"I have loved you," says the LORD. But you say, "How hast thou loved us?" "Is not Esau Jacob's brother?" says the LORD. "Yet I have loved Jacob ³but I have hated Esau; I have laid waste his hill country and left his heritage to jackals of the desert." ⁴If Edom says, "We are shattered but we will rebuild the ruins," the LORD of hosts says, "They may build, but I will tear down, till they are called the wicked country, the people with whom the LORD is angry for ever." ⁵Your own eyes shall see this, and you shall say, "Great is the LORD, beyond the border of Israel!"

The prophecy of Malachi, described as an "oracle," begins rather deceptively with a statement of God's election of Israel over Edom and his fidelity to this choice and to his covenant promises. There is nothing in the opening sentences to reveal that the prophet, in the name of the Lord, will unleash a vigorous indictment of the leaders of Israel. There is a similarity here to the technique of Amos, who pronounced a series of judgments against the enemies of God's people, to which they must have listened with happy complacency until he climaxed the series with oracles against Judah (southern kingdom) and Israel (northern kingdom) (Amos 1 - 2). The fidelity of God in verses 2-5 will be the foil for the stark contrast with the people's infidelity which begins to be condemned in verse 6.

The prophecy proper begins in verse 2 with a pattern of statement - question - response ("I have loved you— How?—Like this . . .") which will reappear in key verses throughout the book to indicate the progress of the argument (1:6; 2:10, 17; 3:7, 13). Hebrew tradition regarded the twin sons of Isaac, Jacob and Esau, as the fathers of the nations Israel and Edom. These two peoples were long-time enemies. The hatred of Israel for Edom had reached a new intensity as a result of the Edomites' cooperation with the invaders in the destruction of Jerusalem (Ps 137:7; Ezek 25:12-14; Obad 11-14). Now Edom, occupying the rough hilly land southeast of the Dead Sea, is suffering invasion at the hands of the Nabateans, a nomadic people of Arabia who had begun to encroach upon their land and would eventually take it over. The Edomites, like the Israelites, will attempt to rebuild what they have lost, but the prophet says the Lord will prevent this because he "hated Esau" (v.3). The Israelites will rejoice at this and proclaim Yahweh's universal lordship (v.5). He showed his power in Babylon; now he manifests it in Edom.

The language of loving and hating brings to the fore the issue of election and predestination. St. Paul uses this text of Malachi to assure his Roman readers that God will not abandon his promises to the Jews even after fulfillment had come in Christ (Rom 9:13). The doctrine of election does not mean God has decided beforehand that some will be saved and others lost. This is often the misreading of Paul's statement in Romans 8:29-30, where he is speaking not from God's point of view in advance nor in terms of individual predestination, but from the viewpoint of the Christian community, which as the people of God has obviously been the recipient of his promises and blessings.

In the present case, too, the prophet is reading the signs of history and concluding that Edom has been "hated." The complete view of election understands that God loves all people (nations and individuals) and gives them the opportunity to decide their eternal destiny on the basis of their response to his love. He loves all, in fact, more than they need, but he does "elect." There is no adequate explanation nor defense for this (nor is one needed) beyond the elusive explanation of love: "It was not because you were more in number than any other people that the Lord set his love upon you and chose you, for you were the fewest of all peoples; but it is because the Lord loves you" (Deut 7:7-8).

SECOND WORD: SNEERING AT THE LORD
1:6-2:9

⁶"A son honors his father, and a servant his master. If then I am a father, where is my honor? And if I am a master, where is my fear? says the LORD of hosts to you, O priests, who despise my name. You say, 'How have we despised thy name?' ⁷By offering polluted food upon my altar. And you say, 'How have we polluted it?' By thinking that the LORD'S table may be despised. ⁸When you offer blind animals in sacrifice, is that no evil? And when you offer those that are lame or sick, is that no evil? Present that to your governor; will he be pleased with you to show you favor? says the LORD of hosts. ⁹"And now entreat the favor of God, that he may

be gracious to us.' With such a gift from your hand, will he show favor to any of you? says the LORD of hosts. [10]Oh, that there were one among you who would shut the doors, that you might not kindle fire upon my altar in vain! I have no pleasure in you, says the LORD of hosts, and I will not accept an offering from your hand. [11]For from the rising of the sun to its setting my name is great among the nations, and in every place incense is offered to my name, and a pure offering; for my name is great among the nations, says the LORD of hosts. [12]But you profane it when you say that the LORD'S table is polluted, and the food for it may be despised. [13]'What a weariness this is,' you say, and you sniff at me, says the LORD of hosts. You bring what has been taken by violence or is lame or sick, and this you bring as your offering! Shall I accept that from your hand? says the LORD. [14]Cursed be the cheat who has a male in his flock, and vows it, and yet sacrifices to the Lord what is blemished; for I am a great King, says the LORD of hosts, and my name is feared among the nations.
2   "And now, O priests, this command is for you. [2]If you will not listen, if you will not lay it to heart to give glory to my name, says the LORD of hosts, then I will send the curse upon you and I will curse your blessings; indeed I have already cursed them, because you do not lay it to heart. [3]Behold, I will rebuke your offspring, and spread dung upon your faces, the dung of your offerings, and I will put you out of my presence. [4]So shall you know that I have sent this command to you, that my covenant with Levi may hold, says the LORD of hosts. [5]My covenant with him was a covenant of life and peace, and I gave them to him, that he might fear; and he feared me, he stood in awe of my name. [6]True instruction was in his mouth, and no wrong was found on his lips. He walked with me in peace and uprightness, and he turned many from iniquity. [7]For the lips of a priest should guard knowledge, and men should seek instruction from his mouth, for he is the messenger of the LORD of hosts.

⁸But you have turned aside from the way; you have caused many to stumble by your instruction; you have corrupted the covenant of Levi, says the LORD of hosts, ⁹and so I make you despised and abased before all the people, inasmuch as you have not kept my ways but have shown partiality in your instruction."

The dialogue pattern is more complicated in the oracle beginning with verse 6. Yahweh's opening statement involves a question: If a son honors his father, why am I, your father, not honored by you? The people then ask how they have "despised" his name. The priests are probably honestly surprised to hear that they are not devoted to the Temple worship; they are faithful to it day after day. But religious practices can be performed by rote and even superstitiously before the decline is noticed, and that seems to be what has happened here.

Gradually the priests have grown tolerant of impure victims for sacrifice (1:7-8), allowing the people to bring defective animals in disobedience to the clear injunction of the Mosaic Law (Lev 22:20-25; Deut 15:21; 17:1). Familiarity with the Temple (and thus with the Lord) has bred contempt. The people would not think of giving such meat to the governor (1:8) who oversees this part of the world for the Persians. So severe is the condemnation of cultic practices that Yahweh says it would be better if the doors to the new Temple were closed (1:10)! The very idea that Yahweh might prefer no sacrifices to the ones they were offering, and that he might want to shut up his dwelling place on earth would have been a terrific jolt to Jewish sensibilities.

From this the argument moves to the famous and controversial passage about the "pure offering" that contrasts with the "polluted" offerings being presented in Jerusalem (1:11). This sacrifice, offered everywhere ("from the rising of the sun to its setting"), is to be understood either as a present reality or something to be expected with the messianic fulfillment. If it is meant as a present reality, it may refer to the Jewish sacrifices being offered by Yahwists living outside Israel in the Diaspora (Dispersion), especially those still in Babylon; or more likely, it refers to pagan sacrifices and makes the cutting point that even these are better than the current Temple offerings. But it is difficult to see how these sacrifices, either Jewish or pagan, could be described as both pure and universal. These are attributes to be expected in the messianic future, when both Jews and Gentiles are envisioned as joining in a pure act of worship fulfilling and perfecting the Mosaic ritual. Catholic tradition, expressed first by the early Fathers of the Church (beginning with Justin) and eventually by the Council of Trent, understands the "pure offering" as fulfilled by the Christian Eucharist, the ritual celebration of the sacrifice of Jesus the Messiah.

After mentioning this pure offering, Yahweh reiterates the strictures against current Temple worship. He talks about "weariness" and "sniffing" (1:13). There is a liturgical weariness that sets in when worship becomes a mere matter of duty and perseverance. Fervor and imagination drift away or are crushed out by legalists. Those who remain faithful to worship in these conditions (and undoubtedly there remained many among the Israelites of Malachi's time) may worship even better because of the adversity, but it is also tempting to relax in the rut. Then, probably without any consciousness of it, the worshiper is effectively sniffing or sneering at the Lord. It is the action rather than the interior offering that has become all-important, and God is being treated impersonally, like an idol.

After having exposed the corruption, Yahweh makes appeal for conversion: lay this command to heart and give glory to my name (2:2). Otherwise, he says, I will "curse your blessings," or "of your blessing I will make a curse" (NAB)—a terrible warning: the implication is that by their present conduct the priests' ministry is not only ineffective, it is destructive. "I will rebuke your offspring" (2:3) is a

threat to put an end to the priestly dynasty. The final word
of this threat may also be read as "arm" or "shoulder";
in the sense that the Lord is threatening to deprive the
priests of their legitimate share (shoulder; Deut 18:3) of the
sacrificial food. Rather the dung of the sacrificial animals
will be thrown in the faces of the priests.

The patriarch Levi, the founder of the priestly order,
is idealized as their forefather in the worship of God (2:4).
He was bound to the Lord by a special covenant, to which
he remained faithful. He gave true *torah* (the word for
"law," translated here as "instruction": 2:6), faithfully
transmitting the Law and giving appropriate interpretation
(Deut 31:9-13). This is a foreshadowing of the procedure
of Ezra and the Levites when he put his reform into effect:
"They read from the book, from the law of God, clearly;
and they gave the sense, so that the people understood
the reading" (Neh 8:8). Malachi speaks to his contemporaries: you should be like Levi; it is the sacred duty of the
priest to live a model life, "guard knowledge" (2:7), and
serve as God's messenger. Revelation of God's message
formerly belonged to the prophets; now everything is in the
hands of the priests. This centralization contributed to the
abuse, leading to "partiality in your instruction (*torah*),"
tailoring the Law.

THIRD WORD: DIVORCE AND COVENANT
2:10-16

[10]Have we not all one father? Has not one God created
us? Why then are we faithless to one another, profaning
the covenant of our fathers? [11]Judah has been faithless,
and abomination has been committed in Israel and in
Jerusalem; for Judah has profaned the sanctuary of the
LORD, which he loves, and has married the daughter
of a foreign god. [12]May the LORD cut off from the tents
of Jacob, for the man who does this, any to witness or
answer, or to bring an offering to the LORD of hosts!

> [13]And this again you do. You cover the LORD'S altar with tears, with weeping and groaning because he no longer regards the offering or accepts it with favor at your hand. [14]You ask, "Why does he not?" Because the LORD was witness to the covenant between you and the wife of your youth, to whom you have been faithless, though she is your companion and your wife by covenant. [15]Has not the one God made and sustained for us the spirit of life? And what does he desire? Godly offspring. So take heed to yourselves, and let none be faithless to the wife of his youth. [16]"For I hate divorce, says the LORD the God of Israel, and covering one's garment with violence, says the LORD of hosts. So take heed to yourselves and do not be faithless."

The questioning in verse 10 signals a new movement and a change of thought. It is not only the priests who have let the glory of the Lord fade in Judah. The prophet attacks the practice of divorce that has been allowed to grow up (vv.14-16). Only the men were able to divorce under the Mosaic Law (Deut 24:1; Hos 2:4), so the strictures are directed against them. They have put aside their Jewish wives and married foreign women who worship other gods (v.11). This sermon of Malachi evidently had no more than partial effect; it will take the severe reforms of Ezra within a few decades to stop the abuse completely (Ezra 9 - 10).

A profound understanding of the marriage bond emerges in these verses. In earlier Israelite history, the wife was considered the property of her husband, something that belonged to him along with the rest of his goods (Ex 20:17); divorce is understandable. But now marriage is seen as a covenant: "She is your companion and your wife by covenant" (v.14). Disregard for the marriage is a breaking of this covenant and also a profaning of the Lord's covenant with Israel. Infidelity to one's covenanted wife is equivalent to profaning the Temple (v.11). The depth of this ancient understanding of marriage makes a telling contrast with a prevalent modern concept of marriage as a mere civil contract. A contract deals with things or with carefully detailed procedures protected by conditions and a default clause. If the terms of the contract are broken, it is rendered void for the other party. But a covenant is between persons and binds them in relationship. The agreement and the obligations can be stated in broad outline, but their disregard does not break the bond. The union remains, even though it may be profaned (Mk 10:2-10). The witness to the covenant of marriage is the living Lord; he regards it as integral to his covenant with the whole people of Israel (v.14).

The prophet sees the practice of divorce as the principal cause of the people's suffering. It is an infringement of the covenant which makes the prescribed sacrifices meaningless. Verse 15, as convoluted as it is, grounds the idea of covenant unity in the unity of God. God "hates divorce," whether of married partners or of those bound together in other ways; he is against the violence that breaks into the unity which has its source in God (v.16). Before Israel can offer a fitting sacrifice, there must be a new commitment to the covenant; the prophet understands that for this there is the prerequisite of purification of the covenant people by returning to unity of spirit and of worship— which in turn means separating from whatever or whoever is not part of the covenant with Yahweh.

FOURTH WORD: THE GOD OF JUSTICE
2:17 - 3:6

17You have wearied the LORD with your words. Yet you say, "How have we wearied him?" By saying, "Every one who does evil is good in the sight of the LORD, and he delights in them." Or by asking, "Where is the God of justice?"

3 "Behold I send my messenger to prepare the way before me, and the Lord whom you seek will suddenly come to his temple; the messenger of the covenant in whom you delight, behold, he is coming, says the LORD of hosts. ²But who can endure the day of his coming, and who can stand when he appears?

"For he is like a refiner's fire and like fullers' soap; ³he will sit as a refiner and purifier of silver, and he will purify the sons of Levi and refine them like gold and silver, till they present right offerings to the LORD. ⁴Then the offering of Judah and Jerusalem will be pleasing to the LORD as in the days of old and as in former years.

⁵"Then I will draw near to you for judgment; I will be a swift witness against the sorcerers, against the adulterers, against those who swear falsely, against those who oppress the hireling in his wages, the widow and the orphan, against those who thrust aside the sojourner, and do not fear me, says the LORD of hosts.

⁶"For I the LORD do not change; therefore you, O sons of Jacob, are not consumed.

This new exchange focuses on the question of God's justice. Why, the people say, do the wicked always prosper while we, the good, must suffer? The prophet's answer will be not that God lets rain fall on just and unjust alike (Mt 5:45) but that the people do not recognize their own evil. The God of justice is present. You have not seen him because of your sins. You would not be able to endure the clarifying light of the Lord's coming (3:2).

The first verse of Chapter Three was immortalized for Christians by Mark's use of it to refer to John the Baptist, the precursor of Jesus (Mk 1:2). It may also be an unnamed source for Luke's portrayal of the arrival of Jesus in the Temple at the time of the presentation (Lk 2:22). The "messenger of the covenant" will fulfill a role of the priests (Mal 2:7) as he introduces the climactic day of divine judgment. A later writer, dissatisfied with the ambiguity of the references, identified the messenger with the returning Elijah (4:5).

From Amos on, the day of the Lord had been announced as a time of judgment, bearing woe for the wicked (Amos 5:18-20; Joel 2:1-2). Malachi now reminds his readers that the abuses of the Jerusalem liturgy will finally be punished and the priests will be purified to offer a pure offering (3:3; see 1:11). The divine judgment will fall on sorcerers and adulterers, and (here he speaks like the prophets of old) on those guilty of social injustice: oppression and cheating of the poor and the weak (3:5). The pure offering can come only from those who are universally just as is the Lord.

To conclude this section, the Lord answers the question with which it began (2:17: "Where is the God of justice?") with a decisive proclamation: "I the Lord do not change" (3:6). Yahweh is indeed true, firm, trustworthy; he does not change his norms, as the priests do (2:9), to accommodate the wicked. But he is faithful in a deeper sense, true to the covenant he has carved with his people. Because of this faithfulness, "You are not consumed" (3:6). God knew the character of his people when he chose them and committed himself to them. He is not surprised by their sinfulness and does not need to react with vengeance. He can bide his time, giving them a chance to hear his voice and return. Perhaps the reference to his people as "sons of Jacob" is meant to remind them that they are like their forefather, who began as a deceiver and supplanter (Gen 25; 27). Yahweh is their heavenly father; unlike the people (2:11) he is faithful to the covenant promises. He bides his time for their sake, but one day there will be an accounting.

FIFTH WORD: FULL TITHES
3:7-12

> [7]From the days of your fathers you have turned aside from my statutes and have not kept them. Return to me, and I will return to you, says the LORD of hosts. But you

say, 'How shall we return?' ⁸Will man rob God? Yet you
are robbing me. But you say, 'How are we robbing thee?'
In your tithes and offerings. ⁹You are cursed with a curse,
for you are robbing me; the whole nation of you. ¹⁰Bring
the full tithes into the storehouse, that there may be
food in my house; and thereby put me to the test, says
the LORD of hosts, if I will not open the windows of
heaven for you and pour down for you an overflowing
blessing. ¹¹I will rebuke the devourer for you, so that
it will not destroy the fruits of your soil; and your vine
in the field shall not fail to bear, says the LORD of
hosts. ¹²Then all nations will call you blessed, for you
will be a land of delight, says the LORD of hosts.

The priests and people have complained that Yahweh
is not a God of justice because he lets the wicked thrive,
particularly the enemies of Israel (2:17). After stating very
clearly in Yahweh's name that the Lord is indeed a just God
who will demand recompense on the day of judgment, the
prophet reveals the kinds of evil God's own people in Jerusalem will have to answer for. The sins of the people in this
section balance the listing of the priests' offenses in 1:6 - 2:9.
Deeds are highlighted here, sinful words in the following
part (3:13 - 4:3).

"How shall we return?" (v.7) is a mock-innocent question, implying that there has never been a departure. The
departure, further questioning reveals, has been in the
withholding of proper tithes and offerings ("robbing
God") from the Temple worship. Two points are worthy
of note. The notion that God is "robbed" when the proper
tithes and offerings are withheld indicates a very different
sense of perspective from an earlier time, when God dis-
dained these offerings as unneeded either because they did
not come from a pure heart (Amos 5:21-22; Isa 43:23) or
because all the world already belongs to the Lord (Ps
50:7-15). Secondly, the tithes are required even though they
will benefit the priests (Num 18:24-32) who because of their

sins do not deserve support. The sins of the priests do not exonerate the people from doing their part in the public worship of Yahweh.

After the curse comes the promise: if you return to me by giving the due offerings, I will "pour down on you an overflowing blessing." Verse 10 is often invoked in support of the practice of tithing in Catholic parishes (five per cent for the parish, five percent for personal charities, world mission, diocesan appeals), not as a "law," but as a helpful biblical norm for concretizing one's devotion to the Lord's kingship (Mt 6:33). The "devourer" in verse 11 is probably the locust (Joel 1:4). All of these blessings of obedience will make Israel a "land of delight" (v.12).

SIXTH WORD: A BOOK OF REMEMBRANCE 3:13 - 4:3 (3:13-21 NAB)

¹³"Your words have been stout against me, says the LORD. Yet you say, 'How have we spoken against thee?' ¹⁴You have said, 'It is vain to serve God. What is the good of our keeping his charge or of walking as in mourning before the LORD of hosts? ¹⁵Henceforth we deem the arrogant blessed; evildoers not only prosper but when they put God to the test they escape.'"

¹⁶Then those who feared the LORD spoke with one another; the LORD heeded and heard them, and a book of remembrance was written before him of those who feared the LORD and thought on his name. ¹⁷"They shall be mine, says the LORD of hosts, my special possession on the day when I act, and I will spare them as a man spares his son who serves him. ¹⁸Then once more you shall distinguish between the righteous and the wicked, between one who serves God and one who does not serve him.

4 "For behold, the day comes, burning like an oven, when all the arrogant and all evildoers will be stubble;

the day that comes shall burn them up, says the LORD
of hosts, so that it will leave them neither root nor branch.
²But for you who fear my name the sun of righteousness
shall rise, with healing in its wings. You shall go forth
leaping like calves from the stall. ³And you shall tread
down the wicked, for they will be ashes under the soles
of your feet, on the day when I act, says the LORD
of hosts.

The people are not going to be let off lightly for their
complaint that God is not just. They were thinking of the
wickedness of others while overlooking their own sins.
The preceding section called attention to their deeds
("robbing"); this one mentions their hostile words, precisely
the charge that God does not punish the wicked. It is the
age-old problem of evil, and we have already seen that
Yahweh explains his tolerance in view of the judgment that
will come at its proper time on the eschatological day of
the Lord.

Those who fear the Lord, that is, show their reverence
for him by just deeds and faithful words, will find their
names written in the "book of remembrance" (3:16). This
heavenly ledger is a traditional symbol in Israel (Ex 32:32;
Isa 4:3). The language of the covenant, recalled several
times throughout the Book of Malachi, appears again with
mention of the people as Yahweh's "special possession"
(3:17; Ex 19:5).

A reader comparing translations or using a commentary
needs to be alerted to the fact that there are verse discrepancies after Malachi 3:18. The RSV, following the
Greek Septuagint, begins a fourth chapter at this point.
Translations following the Hebrew (e.g., NAB) have no
fourth chapter; its verses appear as additional verses of
Chapter Three (3:19-24).

Metaphorical language, almost apocalyptic, describes
the punishment of the wicked on the day of judgment (4:1).
They will be like "stubble" (4:1), like "ashes" (4:3), burnt
in the oven of judgment until neither root nor branch

remains. But the just will feel the healing rays of the "sun of righteousness" (4:2). The imagery is probably borrowed from the worship of the sun-god, especially in Egypt where it was portrayed by a winged solar disc. The coming of righteousness, a healing dawn of deliverance and joy, calls to mind the themes of Zechariah's canticle (Lk 1:68-79). The prophet closes his message with a strong reference to the fact that the Lord, criticized for inaction and excessive tolerance of evil, can and will take action when the appointed time comes (4:3).

POSTSCRIPT
4:4-6 (3:22-24 NAB)

> 4"Remember the law of my servant Moses, the statutes and ordinances that I commanded him at Horeb for all Israel.
> 5"Behold, I will send you Elijah the prophet before the great and terrible day of the LORD comes. 6And he will turn the hearts of fathers to their children and the hearts of children to their fathers, lest I come and smite the land with a curse."

The final three verses of the book are composed of two appendices attached to the original prophecy of Malachi. Verse 4 is a call for fidelity to the Law of Moses intended as an overall concluding admonition to the collection of the twelve Minor Prophets, which ends with the close of Malachi. The editor looks all the way back to the making of the covenant at Horeb (= Sinai), instructing the reader to understand all these later writings as further expressions or applications of the promises and admonitions given there.

Still later, another editor was dissatisfied with the anonymity of the precursor announced in 3:1. He identified the coming messenger with Elijah whose sudden disappearance (2 Kgs 2:11) gave rise to the expectation that he had been taken away by God to be held in readiness for a later mission. It is questionable whether the author of Malachi 3:1 had a specific individual in mind, but the identification with Elijah caught the imagination of later Jewish tradition. The Synoptics (Mk 9:10-13; Mt 11:14; 17:10-13; Lk 1:17) see John the Baptist as fulfilling Elijah's role. The mission of Elijah in 4:5-6 is not just to prepare the Temple for the Lord's coming as in 3:1, but to prepare the whole land by restoring domestic peace.

At a still later stage of the transmission, the rabbis saw to it that verse 5 was repeated after verse 6 so that the collection of the twelve prophets would not end on a note of doom. Though it is not this way in the Hebrew text, the tradition still influences modern editions. The New American Bible repeats verse 5 in italics after verse 6 as an appropriate linking verse between the Old Testament and the New Testament.

After having read the text and commentary together, the reader is urged to take up the biblical text alone and read it through at one sitting, paying attention now to the question-and-answer technique that links the carefully structured sections and moves the thought along. Attentive to the original setting, one can hear the prophetic voice challenging the same sort of laxity in public exercise of religion today. The promise of blessing for faithfulness still holds.

Bibliography

R. L. Braun, "Malachi: A Catechism for Times of Disappointment," *CurrTM* 4 (October, 1977) 297-303.

G. Denzer, *The Books of Haggai, Zechariah, Malachi, Joel*, pages 25-34.

J. Fischer, "Notes on the Literary Form and Message of Malachi," *CBQ* 34 (July, 1972) 315-20.

J. Fischer, "Understanding Malachi," *BT* no. 66 (April, 1973) 1173-1177.

J. Swetnam, "Mal 1,ll: An Interpretation," *CBQ* 31 (April, 1969) 200-209.

Historical Supplement:
Nehemiah and Ezra

HISTORICAL SUPPLEMENT: NEHEMIAH AND EZRA

THE COMPLACENCY and spiritual deterioration denounced by Malachi began to be redressed within a few years by help from an outside source. News of the fading fervor of the descendants of the returned exiles reached Jews still living in Babylon. It stirred into action two reformers who would have decisive influence on the future of Judaism: Nehemiah and Ezra. The story of these two men is scattered through the two books named after them, books originally considered a single work (by the historian who also wrote 1 and 2 Chronicles). Though the Books of Ezra and Nehemiah are treated in Volume 13 of this commentary series, the history surrounding these two figures must be summarized here to complete the picture of postexilic Judah needed for an understanding of the books studied in this volume.

The chronology of the work of Nehemiah and Ezra is hard to decipher because the writer of this history, living a hundred or so years after the events, was himself confused about some of the information handed down to him. The biblical data has it that Ezra the scribe went to Jerusalem in the seventh year of the Persian ruler Artaxerxes. Nehemiah also received his commission from a king of the same name in the twentieth year of his reign (Neh 2:1). If the king in question in both cases is Artaxerxes I Longimanus (465-425 B.C.), Ezra would have arrived in Jerusalem in 458 B.C. (Ezra 7:7) and Nehemiah would have received his commission in 445 B.C. The trouble with this sequence is that Ezra's work of religious reform presupposes Nehemiah's work of completion of the wall of Jerusalem, stabilizing of the population, and stamping out abuses connected with the Temple and the Sabbath.

Most scholars today agree that the sequence Ezra-Nehemiah is not the true one. Ezra followed Nehemiah; otherwise he was a miserable failure (Jerusalem was in a terrible state when Nehemiah arrived) and would not have been remembered as a second Moses in rabbinic tradition. Two solutions have been proposed: 1) the "seventh" year of Artaxerxes is a scribal mistake for "thirty-seventh" year, which means that Ezra's arrival really took place in 428 B.C. (instead of 458); 2) the Artaxerxes in question is not Artaxerxes I but Artaxerxes II Mnemon (404-359 B.C.), in which case the "seventh year" would fall in 397 B.C. In what follows we will not choose between these two hypotheses, but simply assume that Nehemiah is the forerunner of Ezra.

Nehemiah

As Nehemiah describes it, the impetus for his mission came from news brought from Judah about the plight of the inhabitants of Jerusalem and the disrepair of the city wall (Neh 1:2-3). In his important position as cupbearer to the king, Nehemiah was able to gain royal support and funds to pursue his plan of rebuilding the city of his ancestors (Neh 2:5-9). Even this support would have been insufficient for someone without Nehemiah's iron-willed determination and courage. The worst obstacle he encountered was the hostility of Judah's neighbors, particularly the Samaritans, who stood to lose by the restoration of Jewish hopes in Jerusalem.

The Samaritans had hampered the original plans of restoration under Zerubbabel in the early years of the return from Babylon. They were able to postpone the building of the new Temple from 538 B.C. to 520 B.C., when Haggai and Zechariah were able finally to rouse the returnees into action. The fault was not all on the Samaritans' side. They considered themselves followers of the Mosaic Law and had offered to help in the rebuilding of the Jerusalem Temple but had been rejected (Ezra 4:1-5). The Jews looked upon them as contaminated by intermarriage with foreign peoples introduced into Samaria by the Assyrians. The hostility was still there when Nehemiah arrived, and was to lead eventually to the building of a separate Samaritan temple on Mount Gerizim (later to be destroyed by the Jews). Nehemiah also had to contend with the Ammonites to the east and the Edomites to the south. The leaders of the three neighboring provinces, Sanballat, Tobiah and Geshem, accosted Nehemiah as soon as they heard of his plan to rebuild the wall (Neh 2:19). All were apprehensive about the building of a strong Jewish state and the political and economic penalties this might mean for them.

Nehemiah did not let the attacks of these opponents halt his mission. They tried to accuse him of treason; they threatened to attack him; they undermined the morale of his workers. He had to slow the progress of the building by posting half the workmen as guards; and even the others had to carry a weapon while they worked (Neh 4:16-18). Nothing could quench his intense devotion to the project he interpreted as God's design. To messengers inviting him to a conference (probably a trap), Nehemiah replied: "I am doing a great work and I cannot come down" (Neh 6:3). When he was urged to hide in the Temple, he cried: "Should such a man as I flee? And what man such as I could go into the Temple and live? I will not go in" (Neh 6:11).

The wall was finished in fifty-two days (Neh 6:15). Jerusalem was still badly underpopulated, so Nehemiah persuaded the Jews to cast lots so that one in ten would move into the city (Neh 11:1-2). He remained as governor for twelve years, till 433 B.C., achieving extensive reforms in religion and social justice. He returned to Persia, but after a year or two returned to Jerusalem again to find new abuses of Temple and Sabbath (Neh 13:6-22). He corrected these abuses and made strict rules against the intermarriage of Jews with foreigners, even banishing one of the priests involved in such a marriage (Neh 13:23-31). His reforms laid the groundwork for the more extensive religious reforms of Ezra.

Ezra

Some time after Nehemiah's second mission to Jerusalem Ezra, priest and scribe, was given permission (and supplies) to go from Babylon to Judah to refurbish the Temple and re-establish the ancient liturgical practices (Ezra 7:1-6). We do not know whether Nehemiah was still governor at this time, but the two are not mentioned as being together in Jerusalem.

Ezra is approached immediately with the problem that had vexed Nehemiah and, earlier, Malachi (Mal 2:10-11): the marriage of Jews with foreigners. This intermarriage was viewed as a symbol for all the transgressions of the covenant committed by the returned exiles (Ezra 9:14). Ezra is stricter than Nehemiah, who forbade any such future marriages but allowed those who had already taken foreign spouses to remain married (Neh 13:25). Ezra demanded that those involved in mixed marriages should separate (Ezra 10:10-11). Then at the Feast of Booths celebrating the beginning of the new year, Ezra assembled all the people in Jerusalem to hear the reading of the "book of the law of Moses which the Lord had given to Israel" (Neh 8:1). All stood at attention "from early morning until midday" (v.3). Then they celebrated the feast for seven days, carefully observing the ancient ordinances. Two weeks later the people were assembled again, this time in a spirit of penitence. There was reading from the Law and confession of sin. After a great priestly prayer by Ezra, the people ratified the covenant again: "Because of all this we make a firm covenant and write it, and our princes, our Levites, and our priests set their seal to it" (Neh 9:38).

Ezra's initiative in calling the people of Judah back to normative Mosaic practice and giving them the book of the Law has earned for him the title "the father of Judaism." His reform solidified the work of Nehemiah and provided finally the stable basis the post-exilic community needed. But there were some dangers in his measures. The exclusivism instilled by his rejection of all mixed marriages led to a narrow nationalism (evident, for example, in the prophecies of Obadiah and Joel, the books to be studied next). This trend would be challenged from within the community of Israel by the books of Ruth and Jonah. The emphasis on observance of religious laws would lead eventually to an excessive preoccupation with externals—a problem that Jesus had to confront.

But for the time being the people had been reunited and refocused and their religious observance centered within the ancient tradition of Israel. They had been prepared to withstand the attacks of hostile neighbors and the encroachments of misleading ideologies and practices. A major renewal would not be needed again until the time of the Hasmoneans (2nd century B.C.).

Bibliography

D. M. Bossman, "Ezra's Marriage Reform: Israel Redefined," *BTB* 9 (January, 1979) 32-38.

J. Bright, *A History of Israel*. Philadelphia: Westminster Press, second edition, 1972.

R. J. Coggins. *The Books of Ezra and Nehemiah* (Cambridge Bible Commentary). Cambridge: University Press, 1976.

J. M. Myers, *Ezra-Nehemiah* (Anchor Bible, 14). Garden City: Doubleday, 1965.

H. H. Rowley, "Nehemiah's Mission and Its Background," *BJRL* 37 (1954-1955), 528-66.

Obadiah

OBADIAH

Background

THE BOOK OF OBADIAH is the shortest in the Old Testament and, according to some readers, the most vicious. We know nothing about the identity of the author, except that he was a person filled with bitterness against the Edomites, ancient enemies of his people. The oracle of Obadiah is hard to date because there are ambiguous references to offenses and hostilities that happened at various times in the stormy relationship of Edom and Israel.

The Edomites were a Semitic tribe which folklore associated intimately with the Hebrews: the two peoples were considered descendants of the twin sons of Isaac (Gen 25:23). The Edomites had also been a nomadic people before they settled, about 1300 B.C. (before the Hebrews), southeast of Palestine in a region that would eventually border the land of Judah. In the memory of Israel is the story of Edom's refusal to let the Hebrews pass through their territory when they were traveling from Egypt to Canaan (Num 20:14-21).

When the monarchy had been established in Israel, Saul fought with Edom and other enemy neighbors (1 Sam 14:47) and held them at bay. David conquered them (2 Sam 8:14; 1 Kgs 11:15), opening the way for his son Solomon to establish shipping operations through Ezion-geber on the

Gulf of Aqaba (1 Kgs 9:26-28). But like other things, this ascendancy over Edom began to deteriorate during Solomon's reign. The Edomite prince Hadad came out of hiding in Egypt to lead raids on Israel (1 Kgs 11:14-22). Edom continued to try to shake off the Hebrew yoke after the split of the Kingdom, while the kings of Judah (South) worked to keep the country subjugated. King Jehoshapat controlled the area during his reign (873-849 B.C.), when there was "no king in Edom" (1 Kgs 22:47). The Edomites revolted against his successor, Jehoram (849-842 B.C.), who was not able to control the situation (2 Kgs 8:20-22). Later on King Amaziah (800-783 B.C.) pushed the frontier of Judah as far as Sela (2 Kgs 14:7); his successor Uzziah (783-742 B.C.) was able to open up Ezion-Geber (Elath) on the Gulf of Aqaba (2 Chr 26:2). Edom finally broke free from Judah during the reign of Ahaz (735-715 B.C.; 2 Kgs 16:6).

Edom, like Israel and Judah, fell under the sway of Assyria and then Babylon, paying tribute from the early eighth century on. When the Babylonian invaders under Nebuchadnezzar II took Jerusalem in 587 B.C., Edom took advantage of the opportunity to get even with the Israelites (Ezek 25: 12; 35:5). The Edomites cooperated with the Babylonians, then moved into Judah, setting up a capital at Hebron. The deep resentment this provoked is evident in Lamentations 4:21-22 and Psalm 137:7. There was (understandably) still bad blood between the two nations after Jerusalem's return from Babylon.

Sometime around 500 B.C., or at least before 450, Nabatean nomads from Arabia began to make raids on Edom (Mal 1:2-4). By the last half of the fifth century the Arabs were in control. This pressure combined with the fact that some of their people were already in the Hebron area induced many Edomites to move into southern Judea, into an area that would eventually be called Idumaea: it was the homeland of Herod the Great. Under John Hyrcanus (134-104 B.C.) the Edomites were absorbed by the Jews.

Edom and Earlier Prophets

Obadiah had plenty of fuel from earlier biblical writings for his diatribe against Edom. The prophets are laced with anti-Edom oracles (Amos 1:11-12; Jer 49:7-22; Isa 35:5-17; 63:1-6; Ezek 25:12-14; 35:1-15). There are so many similarities between Jeremiah 49 and the first part of Obadiah that some scholars thought the two books must have been written out of the same historical experience. Now it is evident that Obadiah was written much later. He is adapting an earlier oracle to a later time, either quoting Jeremiah or using a source employed by the earlier prophet. Obadiah then makes his own original contribution in verses 15-21.

The references to the fall of Jerusalem in verses 11-12 place the book at least after 587 B.C. But it can be dated more than a century later, in the mid-fifth century, when the Edomites had been displaced from their homeland. The prophecy of Malachi was written while this ouster was still in process (Mal 1:3-4). The message of Obadiah seems to have been aroused by the sight of this initial punishment of Israel's enemies; it became for the prophet a sign of the final victory of Yahweh over his enemies and the establishment of his kingship on earth.

The vision of Obadiah is not simply a bloodthirsty cry of revenge bursting from Israelite nationalism. The downfall of Edom is understood as the result of its sins; it is a warning for all nations that a day of moral reckoning is coming. Obadiah's strident tones are not out of character in the prophetic literature, and his message of divine kingship in a purified land is in the mainstream of exilic and post-exilic Scripture.

THE FALL OF EDOM
1-7

¹The vision of Obadiah.

Thus says the Lord GOD concerning Edom:
We have heard tidings from the LORD, and a

messenger has been sent among the nations:
"Rise up! let us rise against her for battle!"
²Behold, I will make you small among the nations,
   you shall be utterly despised.
³The pride of your heart has deceived you,
   you who live in the clefts of the rock,
   whose dwelling is high,
who say in your heart,
   "Who will bring me down to the ground?"
⁴Though you soar aloft like the eagle,
   though your nest is set among the stars,
thence I will bring you down, says the LORD.

⁵If thieves came to you,
   if plunderers by night—
   how you have been destroyed!—
   would they not steal only enough for themselves?
If grape gatherers came to you,
   would they not leave gleanings?
⁶How Esau has been pillaged,
   his treasures sought out!
⁷All your allies have deceived you,
   they have driven you to the border;
your confederates have prevailed against you;
your trusted friends have set a trap under you—
   there is no understanding of it.

The news of Edom's downfall before Arab invaders comes like glad tidings to Obadiah and his friends (v.1). Though the long history of animosity is behind this feeling, its more proximate reason is the conduct of the Edomites during Israel's darkest night in 587 B.C. Edom's pride and gloating at the downfall of Judah is associated with the natural environment of Edom (v.3). Edom was dominated by the 45-mile-long range of Mount Seir, with its peaks and plateaus averaging 4800 feet above sea level. The "rock" refers to Sela, the ancient capital of Edom perched high on one of the dominant plateaus. The walls of the cliffs in the region are pocked with small caves and crevices, ideal for hiding people or their treasures (v.6).

The tone of these verses, especially verse 6, is reminiscent of "How are the mighty fallen" in David's lament for Saul and Jonathan (2 Sam 1:19-27) and of the tragic reversal of Jerusalem in Lamentations (1:1; 2:1; 4:1). The fall of Edom is complete. Thieves in the night take only what they can easily carry; grape harvesters were required to leave something for the poor (Lev 19:10; Deut 24:21); but Edom has lost everything (vv.5-6). The irony of betrayal is being built up in these verses. These Arab invaders were thought to be friends of yours, your allies (literally "men of your covenant"), but "your trusted friends have set a trap under you" (v.7).

A BROTHER'S BETRAYAL
8-14

8Will I not on that day, says the LORD,
   destroy the wise men out of Edom,
   and understanding out of Mount Esau?
9And your mighty men shall be dismayed, O Teman,
   so that every man from Mount Esau
      will be cut off by slaughter.
10For the violence done to your brother Jacob,
   shame shall cover you,
   and you shall be cut off for ever.
11On the day that you stood aloof,
   on the day that strangers carried off his wealth,
   and foreigners entered his gates
   and cast lots for Jerusalem,
   you were like one of them.
12But you should not have gloated over the day of
   your brother
   in the day of his misfortune;
you should not have rejoiced over the people of Judah
   in the day of their ruin;

you should not have boasted
in the day of distress.
[13]You should not have entered the gate of my people
in the day of his calamity;
you should not have gloated over his disaster
in the day of his calamity;
you should not have looted his goods
in the day of his calamity.
[14]You should not have stood at the parting of the ways
to cut off his fugitives;
you should not have delivered up his survivors
in the day of distress.

Edom, the descendant of Esau, stood by licking his chops as Judah, descendant of Jacob, was pillaged and dragged away. This was a further act of "violence done to your brother Jacob" (v.10). The wisdom of Edom's sages was proverbial in the East (Job 2:11; Jer 49:7; Bar 3:22-23). But Edom's trust in the Arab neighbors has turned out to be foolishness; on the day of the Lord all of Edom's wisdom will be useless (vv.8-9) because of Esau-Edom's senseless betrayal of his brother, Jacob-Judah. The cutting words in these ironic verses could pierce the conscience of anyone involved in a covenant betrayal: family, marriage, friendship, or those with whom one has shared a covenant meal.

The words "your bread" appear, in fact, in the Hebrew of verse 7, causing difficulty for translators. The RSV solves the problem by translating the passage "your trusted friends" with the meaning of "those who eat your bread" (as in the NAB). Eastern hospitality looks upon table fellowship as establishing an interpersonal bond. Betrayal by one with whom a meal has been shared is a special form of treachery. Psalm 41:9, "Even my bosom friend in whom I trusted, who ate of my bread, has lifted his heel against me," is a commentary on the action of Edom's neighbors toward Edom and of Edom toward Judah, as it was later on the action of Judas (Jn 13:18).

Obadiah's special name for Mount Seir is Mount Esau, which emphasizes again the family relationship of the two peoples. It stands for the whole nation as does Teman, the name of an Edomite city, in verse 9. The repetition of "You should not have" eight times in verses 12-14 provides a plaintive, even dirge-like tone that is in the tradition of the Improperia of the Good Friday services (inspired by Micah; see Micah 6:3). Edom could have been expected to show at least neutrality on the day of Babylon's invasion of Jerusalem. Instead the Edomites cooperated actively, applauding the marauders and sharing in the spoil; and worst of all, blocking the way of escape for the fugitives.

THE DAY OF THE LORD
15-16

> ¹⁵For the day of the LORD is near upon all the nations.
> As you have done, it shall be done to you,
> your deeds shall return on your own head.
> ¹⁶For as you have drunk upon my holy mountain,
> all the nations round about shall drink;
> they shall drink, and stagger,
> and shall be as though they had not been.

There is an evident change of focus with verse 15. From a very particular condemnation of Edom, the vision turns to a proclamation about what all nations can look forward to on the "day of the Lord." Edom is reminded briefly of the principle of retaliation (v.15) adopted from the culture by Israel: ". . . an eye for an eye, a tooth for a tooth" (Exod 21:23-25; Lev 24:17-22). When originally introduced, this was a merciful correction of the earlier practice of overcompensating for injury (for example, murder in return for robbery); Jesus further corrected this by his absolute law of mercy: "I say to you, Do not resist the one who is evil. But if any one strikes you on the right cheek, turn to him the other also" (Mt 5:38-41).

The "you" of verse 16 refers to the people of Judah. They have drunk the cup of the Lord's wrath at the time of the destruction by Babylon; eventually all the rebellious nations will have to drink of the same cup (Jer 25:15-17). A purified remnant of Israel will be protected. This theme we have encountered often in other post-exilic oracles.

RESTORATION
17-21

[17]But in Mount Zion there shall be those that escape,
and it shall be holy;
and the house of Jacob shall possess
their own possessions.
[18]The house of Jacob shall be a fire,
and the house of Joseph a flame,
and the house of Esau stubble;
they shall burn them and consume them,
and there shall be no survivor to the house of Esau;
for the LORD has spoken.
[19]Those of the Negeb shall possess Mount Esau,
and those of the Shephelah the land of the Philistines;
they shall possess the land of Ephraim
and the land of Samaria
and Benjamin shall possess Gilead.
[20]The exiles in Halah who are of the people of Israel
shall possess Phoenicia as far as Zarephath;
and the exiles of Jerusalem who are in Sepharad
shall possess the cities of the Negeb.
[21]Saviors shall go up to Mount Zion to rule Mount Esau;
and the kingdom shall be the LORD'S.

The final verses of the prophecy foresee the restoration of the whole ancient kingdom of Israel, both North (Joseph) and South (Jacob). Judah will no longer be the very restricted area of Jerusalem and its environs, but the kingdom will expand to the frontiers of David's time. The Israelites will reoccupy the Negeb to the south which was encroached upon by Edom during the Exile (reading verse 19 with the NAB: "They shall occupy the Negeb, the mount of Esau . . .".). The people of the Shephelah, the low hill country to the west of Judah, will take over Philistine territory. The northern kingdom, identified by the leading regions of Ephraim and Samaria, will again be incorporated into Israel. Benjamin, just north of Jerusalem, will take over the land of Gilead beyond the Jordan. All of this expresses a vision of a coming universal kingdom when pagan nations will belong to the Lord.

Verse 20 has been the subject of several scholarly disputes over the translation of the first phrase ("The exiles in Halah" - RSV; "The captives of the host" - NAB) and the identity of Sepharad. A satisfactory sense can be made of the RSV if both Halah (see 2 Kgs 17:6) and Sepharad are located in Babylon. Then the prophet is saying that one group of exiles will possess the land along the Mediterranean Sea (Phoenicia as far as Zarephath, a city north of Tyre), another will possess the Negeb. Other identifications of Sepharad include places in Media, Egypt and (especially) in Asia Minor (Sardis: Rev 3:1). In later times the rabbis interpreted this name as Spain. As a result Spanish and Portuguese Jews are still called Sephardim.

The vision ends with the scene of "saviors" ruling on Mount Zion in the name of the Lord (v.21). The word for savior is the same as the word used for the early judges of Israel (Judg 3:9, 15, 31: "deliverer"); here the rulers are Davidic kings. The vindictive threats addressed to Edom in the opening lines of Obadiah must be read within the context of the second part, especially in light of this final verse, where even Edom is included under the universal kingship of Yahweh.

Bibliography

Leslie C. Allen, *The Books of Joel, Obadiah, Jonah and Micah* (New International Commentary on the Old Testament), Grand Rapids: Eerdmans, 1976.

J. R. Lillie, "Obadiah: a Celebration of God's Kingdom," *CurrTM* 6 (February, 1979) 18-22.

G. T. Montague, *The Books of Zephaniah, Nahum, Habbakuk, Lamentations, Obadiah*, pages 98-105.

J. Muilenburg, "Book of Obadiah," *Interpreter's Bible*, Volume 3, pages 578-579.

J. D. W. Watts, *The Books of Joel, Obadiah, Jonah, Nahum. Habbakuk and Zephaniah* (Cambridge Bible Commentary). Cambridge and New York: Cambridge University Press, 1975.

J. D. W. Watts, *Obadiah, A Critical, Exegetical Commentary*, Grand Rapids: Eerdmans, 1969.

Joel

JOEL

Background

THE BOOK OF JOEL is a clear example of the "before" and "after" of a particular prophetic ministry. The first half (1:1-2:17) paints a vivid picture of danger and distress as the land of Judah is invaded by a terrible locust plague, worse than any before. The prophet interprets this as a sign of divine judgment and a warning from God about the coming day of the Lord. Joel urges the people to repentance. In the second part, the prophet reports that the intense prayer of the people has been heard; the locust plague has ended. He presents a vision of the day of the Lord, describing the judgment but emphasizing the outpouring of the spirit of God on the faithful of Yahweh in Jerusalem. Joel is a very good writer. His poetry sparkles with comparisons, concrete detail, contrasts, and timely repetitions.

This book takes us a step further along in the life of post-exilic Israel. It is dated about 400 B.C. The priests are in control, as they have been for some time; there is no mention of governors or kings. The Temple has been restored and is in use. There may even be a reference to the wall built by Nehemiah during his first governorship (445-433 B.C.: Joel 2:7,9). Joel uses material from the prophecies of Malachi and Obadiah: compare Joel 2:11 and Malachi 3:2; Joel 2:32 and Obadiah 17. (The discrepancies in the versification of Joel will be noted in the

133

commentary.) On the other hand, the prophecy can hardly be later than 350 B.C., because it reflects a peaceful political world scene. That peace would be shattered by uprisings against the Persian rulers from within their empire (in Syria, for example, in 345 B.C.) and the takeover by Alexander and the Greeks in 333 B.C.

Joel's prophecy reveals a situation in Jerusalem already quite different from that of Malachi's time about fifty years earlier. Malachi was faced with the laxity of a generation that had grown accustomed to the restored Temple and had allowed the liturgical observance to decline. His stirring challenge was followed rather closely by the coming of Nehemiah and the building of the city wall, and the mission of Ezra with his proclamation of the Law and the imposition of strict marriage laws and other ordinances to purify the people. By Joel's time the people are living a more vigorous liturgical life and have been drawn into a closely-knit worshiping community. When Joel calls for prayer and penance, the response is swift.

The situation of Joel's community had its own inherent dangers. It could easily become isolated, self-centered and ingrown. This does not seem to have happened yet, but there is no universalism in Joel. The outpouring of the spirit is for Israelites, no one else. It will soon be time for the author of the Book of Jonah to shake the people out of their isolationism and complacency and present a more universal vision as the context of Israel's hope. On another plane, they will soon be awakened to the presence of the outside world by the sweeping conquests of Alexander the Great. The effect of this event in the Jewish community will be detected in Second Zechariah.

Part I:
The Plague of Locusts

LOCUST PLAGUE
1:1-12

1 The word of the LORD that came to Joel, the son of Pethuel:

²Hear this, you aged men,
    give ear, all inhabitants of the land!
Has such a thing happened in your days,
    or in the days of your fathers?
³Tell your children of it,
    and let your children tell their children,
    and their children another generation.

⁴What the cutting locust left,
    the swarming locust has eaten.
What the swarming locust left,
    the hopping locust has eaten,
and what the hopping locust left,
    the destroying locust has eaten.

⁵Awake, you drunkards, and weep;
    and wail, all you drinkers of wine,
because of the sweet wine,
    for it is cut off from your mouth.
⁶For a nation has come up against my land,
    powerful and without number;
its teeth are lions' teeth,
    and it has the fangs of a lioness.

⁷It has laid waste my vines,
    and splintered my fig trees;
it has stripped off their bark and thrown it down;
    their branches are made white.

8Lament like a virgin girded with sackcloth
for the bridegroom of her youth.
9The cereal offering and the drink offering are cut off
from the house of the LORD.
The priests mourn,
the ministers of the LORD.
10The fields are laid waste,
the ground mourns;
because the grain is destroyed,
the wine fails,
the oil languishes.

11Be confounded, O tillers of the soil,
wail, O vinedressers,
for the wheat and the barley;
because the harvest of the field has perished.
12The vine withers,
the fig tree languishes.
Pomegranate, palm, and apple,
all the trees of the field are withered;
and gladness fails
from the sons of men.

We know nothing more about Joel than his identification as the son of Pethuel in the opening verse. He is very concerned about the Temple liturgy and may have been a minister of some kind, though he does not speak of himself as a priest. He appeals for the attention of all in the land, and in vivid terms describes a terrible locust plague which has devastated the countryside. He claims it is the worst that anyone living has ever seen and that it is not likely to be believed when future generations hear about it (vv.2-3). However severe was the plague, readers of any age know how it feels when especially harsh suffering comes. It will always seem as if this is the worst on record, worse than anyone else has experienced, and that nothing can effectively soothe the pain.

Four different words are used in verse 4 to identify the locust (see also 2:25). These are probably different stages of development, though not in consecutive order. The locust hatches as a small "hopper" which can begin eating vegetation immediately; and through stages becomes the winged "cutter" for which nothing is out of reach. Locust swarms usually came from the Arabian desert or from the Sudan in Africa and could migrate up to a thousand miles, eating practically everything in their path. The force is compared to a foreign army (v.6). This plague seems to have come late in the growing season, just before the fall harvest which was celebrated by the Feast of Booths, at which time the participants drank heavily of the partly fermented ("sweet") early wine (v.5). Those looking forward mainly to that part of the festival would be affected as well as those with more religious motives. Coming within a few weeks or days of the harvest, the tragedy could well be compared to the death of the bridegroom shortly before the wedding (v.8).

So severe is the resulting shortage of grain and wine that the regular Temple offerings cannot be continued (v.9). This probably entailed also the cessation of the animal sacrifices; there was nothing to feed the two lambs needed daily (2 Kgs 16:15; Ezra 3:3). Only in cases of extreme calamity could this be allowed, for the Temple liturgy was the public sign of normal covenant relations between Yahweh and his people. The fields are described as "mourning," the oil "languishing," while the people lose the feeling of joy and gladness that accompanies the conviction of God's protection and providence (vv.10,12). The contrast of mood is striking in comparison with the happy festival song of another time:

"Thou crownest the year with thy bounty;
   the tracks of thy chariot drip with fatness . . . .
the meadows clothe themselves with flocks,
   the valleys deck themselves with grain,
   they shout and sing together for joy" (Ps 65:11-13).

CALL TO PENANCE
1:13-20

¹³Gird on sackcloth and lament, O priests,
   wail, O ministers of the altar,
Go in, pass the night in sackcloth,
   O ministers of my God!
Because cereal offering and drink offering
   are withheld from the house of your God.

¹⁴Sanctify a fast,
   call a solemn assembly.
Gather the elders
   and all the inhabitants of the land
to the house of the LORD your God;
   and cry to the LORD.

¹⁵Alas for the day!
For the day of the LORD is near,
   and as destruction from the Almighty it comes.

¹⁶Is not the food cut off
   before our eyes,
joy and gladness
   from the house of our God?

¹⁷The seed shrivels under the clods,
   the storehouses are desolate;
the granaries are ruined
   because the grain has failed.
¹⁸How the beasts groan!
   The herds of cattle are perplexed
because there is no pasture for them;
   even the flocks of sheep are dismayed.

¹⁹Unto thee, O LORD, I cry.
For fire has devoured
   the pastures of the wilderness,
and flame has burned
   all the trees of the field.

20Even the wild beasts cry to thee
   because the water brooks are dried up,
and fire has devoured
   the pastures of the wilderness.

Verse 13 begins a call to action. The priests are urged to
call a fast and, to give good example, to wear sackcloth as a
sign of penitential prayer. Usually penances were suspended
at evening, but in extreme cases sackcloth was worn through
the night (2 Sam 12:16; 1 Kgs 21:27). All the people are to
be included in the national plea for God's intervention.
The plague is viewed as a prelude to the day of the Lord
(v.15; see 2:1-11). Israel yearned for this day of vindication,
but with some trepidation, knowing that it would involve
judgment and retribution for evil. The call for prayer and
penance ends with striking repetitions and new images of
universal suffering: seed shrivels, beasts groan, cattle are
perplexed, sheep are dismayed (vv.17-18). "Even the wild
beasts cry to thee" (v.20); how much more should God's
own people?

A DAY OF DARKNESS
2:1-17

2   Blow the trumpet in Zion;
sound the alarm on my holy mountain!
Let all the inhabitants of the land tremble,
   for the day of the LORD is coming, it is near,
2a day of darkness and gloom,
   a day of clouds and thick darkness!
Like blackness there is spread upon the mountains
   a great and powerful people;
their like has never been from of old,
   nor will be again after them
   through the years of all generations.

³Fire devours before them,
  and behind them a flame burns.
The land is like the garden of Eden before them,
  but after them a desolate wilderness,
  and nothing escapes them.

⁴Their appearance is like the appearance of horses,
  and like war horses they run.
⁵As with the rumbling of chariots,
  they leap on the tops of the mountains,
like the crackling of a flame of fire devouring the stubble.
  like a powerful army
  drawn up for battle.

⁶Before them peoples are in anguish,
  all faces grow pale.
⁷Like warriors they charge,
  like soldiers they scale the wall.
They march each on his way,
  they do not swerve from their paths.
⁸They do not jostle one another,
  each marches in his path;
they burst through the weapons
  and are not halted.
⁹They leap upon the city,
  they run upon the walls;
they climb up into the houses,
  they enter through the windows like a thief.

¹⁰The earth quakes before them,
  the heavens tremble.
The sun and the moon are darkened,
  and the stars withdraw their shining.
¹¹The LORD utters his voice
  before his army,
for his host is exceedingly great;
  he that executes his word is powerful.
For the day of the LORD is great and very terrible;
  who can endure it?

12"Yet even now," says the LORD,
   "return to me with all your heart,
with fasting, with weeping, and with mourning;
13and rend your hearts and not your garments."
Return to the LORD, your God,
   for he is gracious and merciful,
slow to anger, and abounding in steadfast love,
   and repents of evil.
14Who knows whether he will not turn and repent,
   and leave a blessing behind him,
a cereal offering and a drink offering
   for the LORD, your God?

15Blow the trumpet in Zion;
   sanctify a fast;
call a solemn assembly;
   16gather the people.
Sanctify the congregation;
   assemble the elders;
gather the children,
   even nursing infants.
Let the bridegroom leave his room,
   and the bride her chamber.

17Between the vestibule and the altar
   let the priests, the ministers of the LORD, weep
and say, "Spare thy people, O LORD,
   and make not thy heritage a reproach,
   a byword among the nations.
Why should they say among the peoples,
   'Where is their God?'"

The prophet calls for a blast on the *shophar*, the ram's horn, to announce the day of the Lord (v.1: see Hos 5:8; Jer 4:5). Much in these verses is a second description of the locust invasion, but with more emphasis on end-time symbolism and on the comparison to an invading army. The vivid descriptions of this chapter influenced Revelation

9:3-11, which pictures eschatological punishment in terms of a locust plague.

Amos had described the day of the Lord as "darkness and not light" (Amos 5:20); here the darkness is caused by the clouds of insects blocking out the sun (v.2). Nothing stops the onslaught of the locusts. They are a marauding army with the power to turn the Garden of Eden into a desert (v.3). The locusts climb the wall of the city and crawl through the open windows of the houses (vv.7-9). Even the cosmos is involved: the earth quakes, the skies are darkened (v.10), traditional imagery for the eschatological judgment (Mk 13:24-25).

In the familiar language of the ancient prophets, Joel calls for a return to the Lord (vv.12-13; see Hos 2:9; Jer 3:12-14). The exterior signs of repentance are mentioned, but it is the interior spirit of penance that is sought. What Joel is calling for was familiar from Jeremiah as a new covenant of the heart (Jer 31:31-34) and from Ezekiel as a new heart and new spirit (Ezek 36:24-28). The Church adopts this admonition for the Ash Wednesday liturgy: "Rend your hearts and not your garments!" (v.13). The hope of being received is based on Yahweh's fidelity to his covenant. If the prodigal son returns, the Father will be there to receive him (Lk 15:20). The priests are to organize a penitential crusade involving all the people (v.15). The situation is so serious that even the babies are not spared, nor the newlyweds who were ordinarily exempt from public service (v.16; see Deut 24:5). The priests stand in the space between the Temple porch and the altar of holocausts to mourn publicly for the sins of the whole people. The appeal is to Yahweh's enlightened self-interest: if you do not help us, the Gentiles will doubt your power to protect us (v.17).

Part II:
The New Age

REJOICE IN THE LORD
2:18-27

¹⁸Then the LORD became jealous for his land,
and had pity on his people.
¹⁹The LORD answered and said to his people,
"Behold, I am sending to you
grain, wine, and oil,
and you will be satisfied;
and I will no more make you
a reproach among the nations.

²⁰"I will remove the northerner far from you,
and drive him into a parched and desolate land,
his front into the eastern sea,
and his rear into the western sea;
the stench and foul smell of him will rise,
for he has done great things.

²¹"Fear not, O land;
be glad and rejoice,
for the LORD has done great things!
²²Fear not, you beasts of the field,
for the pastures of the wilderness are green;
the tree bears its fruit,
the fig tree and vine give their full yield.

²³"Be glad, O sons of Zion,
and rejoice in the LORD, your God;
for he has given the early rain for your vindication,
he has poured down for you abundant rain,
the early and the latter rain, as before.

²⁴"The threshing floors shall be full of grain,
the vats shall overflow with wine and oil.

25I will restore to you the years
  which the swarming locust has eaten,
the hopper, the destroyer, and the cutter,
  my great army, which I sent among you.

26"You shall eat in plenty and be satisfied,
  and praise the name of the LORD your God,
  who has dealt wondrously with you.
And my people shall never again be put to shame.
27You shall know that I am in the midst of Israel,
  and that I, the LORD, am your God
  and there is none else.
And my people shall never again
  be put to shame.

Verse 18 marks the turning point of the book. The first part has been a description of the plague as a sign of the coming judgment of God and a plea for penance and prayer to change Yahweh's intent. The threat has now been averted, the plague is over and the rains have come (v.23). These verses describe Yahweh's answer to the prayer of his people. He became "jealous" for them and had pity (v.18). The blessings of prosperity which had disappeared are now restored: grain, wine and oil (v.19; see Deut 7:13; Hos 2:10). Repeated several times is the theme that God's intervention takes away the "reproach" of the people (vv.19, 23, 26, 27). They do have a powerful God who can protect them and intends to save them. His tolerance of the plague was, like the Exile, no sign of weakness or unconcern on his part.

The "northerner" (v.20) is best explained as a figurative description of the locust invasion. Israel had been plagued by enemies from the north, particularly the Mesopotamian powers, and invasion from the north had become a symbol for the eschatological battle (Ezek 38:6,15). The locusts begin to die out in the "parched land" of the Negeb; they fall into the "eastern sea," the Dead Sea, and the "western sea," the Mediterranean (v.20).

The return of well-being is described above all in terms of rain, abundant and at the proper time: early rain for the fall planting, late rain just before spring harvest (v.23). From this bounty comes the return to strength and beauty of the animals and the fields. This is "for your vindication," a proof that God is present in the midst of Israel (v.27). The phrase of verse 23 can also be rendered "He has given you the teacher of justice" (NAB); in this reading it is a messianic promise. This is the origin of the title "Teacher of Righteousness" of the founder of the Qumran community in the second century B.C. The strong affirmation of Yahweh's uniqueness and his dedication to his people at the end of this section (v.27) is a decisive reply to the taunt of verse 17.

THE OUTPOURING OF THE SPIRIT
2:28-32 (3:1-5 NAB)

> 28"And it shall come to pass afterward,
>   that I will pour out my spirit on all flesh;
> your sons and your daughters shall prophesy,
>   your old men shall dream dreams,
>   and your young men shall see visions.
> 29Even upon the menservants and maidservants
>   in those days, I will pour out my spirit.
> 30"And I will give portents in the heavens and on the earth, blood and fire and columns of smoke. 31The sun shall be turned to darkness, and the moon to blood, before the great and terrible day of the LORD comes. 32And it shall come to pass that all who call upon the name of the LORD shall be delivered; for in Mount Zion and in Jerusalem there shall be those who escape, as the LORD has said, and among the survivors shall be those whom the LORD calls.

This section is 3:1-5 in versions following the division in the Hebrew text. These few verses are well known to

Christians because of their use in Peter's Pentecost sermon in Acts 2:17-21. The whole of the section except for part of the final verse is used in the New Testament text. Here the emphasis is on the eschatological day of the Lord as a time of blessing. Though the prophet is speaking of universal blessings only in the sense of the whole of Israel, St. Peter understands these words in their fulfilled sense to apply to all peoples.

The most striking sign of the messianic age is the pouring out of the spirit of the Lord on all indiscriminately (vv.28-29). The Hebrews knew the spirit as a gift for special agents of divine mandate and judgment. Judges, kings and prophets were given a gift of the spirit (Judg 6:34; 1 Sam 16:13; Ezek 11:5). The spirit that was on Moses was shared with the seventy elders chosen to help him minister to the people (Num 11:17). He expressed the wish that all the people might possess the spirit (11:29). This will happen, says Joel as he echoes earlier prophets, in the fulfillment time in the day of the Lord (Isa 32:15; Ezek 36:26-27). Peter's sermon identifies the resurrection and ascension of Jesus as the occasion for the general bestowing of this gift: "Being therefore exalted at the right hand of God, and having received from the Father the promise of the Holy Spirit, he has poured out this which you see and hear" (Acts 2:33).

"Those who escape" (see Obad 17) are synonymous with "those whom the Lord calls" in the parallel construction of verse 32. Earlier prophetic literature speaks of Israel's survival as a "remnant," which the Lord would scatter to the winds (Ezek 5:10). After it has been chastized (Jer 15:9), the remnant will return and be restored to the land of Israel (Isa 10:22; 11:11; Zech 8:6-8). Then it will occupy not only its own territory but the land of its enemies (Zeph 2:7-9).

THE VALLEY OF JEHOSHAPHAT
3:1-8 (4:1-8 NAB)

3 "For behold, in those days and at that time, when I restore the fortunes of Judah and Jerusalem, ²I will gather all the nations and bring them down to the valley of Jehoshaphat, and I will enter into judgment with them there, on account of my people and my heritage Israel, because they have scattered them among the nations, and have divided up my land, ³and have cast lots for my people, and have given a boy for a harlot, and have sold a girl for wine, and have drunk it.

⁴"What are you to me, O Tyre and Sidon, and all the regions of Philistia? Are you paying me back for something? If you are paying me back, I will requite your deed upon your own head swiftly and speedily. ⁵For you have taken my silver and my gold, and have carried my rich treasures into your temples. ⁶You have sold the people of Judah and Jerusalem to the Greeks, removing them far from their own border. ⁷But now I will stir them up from the place to which you have sold them, and I will requite your deed upon your own head. ⁸I will sell your sons and your daughters into the hand of the sons of Judah, and they will sell them to the Sabeans, to a nation far off; for the LORD has spoken."

After portraying the future blessings of the people of Israel on the day of the Lord, the prophet turns for the first time to dealing with the enemies of his people. The narrow nationalism of this post-exilic time is evident as Joel envisions messianic glory only for the people of Judah (v. 1). The gathering of the nations for judgment (and defeat) is a theme of the pre-exilic prophet Zephaniah (Zeph 3:8), but it will be only the enemies of Israel who are tried at the Valley of Jehoshaphat (v.2). The name of this valley means "Yahweh judges": it is later called the Valley of Decision (v.14). Popular imagination has since the fourth century A.D. identified this symbolic place with the Kidron Valley between Jerusalem and the Mount of Olives. Yahweh brings the enemies of his people together to seek vindication. He is personally involved: *my* people, *my* heritage, *my* land (v.2). Many Hebrews were still in foreign exile at this time. They had been treated shabbily by their conquerors, who showed their lack of respect by selling and trading them as slaves for momentary gratification ("given a boy for a harlot": v.3). A prose insert (vv.4-8) in this poetry singles out the Phoenicians (Tyre and Sidon) and the Philistines, notorious for their traffic in slaves (Amos 1:6-10; Ezek 27:13; 2 Chr 21:16-17). They sold the Israelites to the Greeks who took them far away to Ionia in the northwest; their own sons and daughters will be sold to the Sabeans in the land of Sheba on the southern tip of Arabia, a land that is just as far away from Palestine in the opposite direction.

Conquering armies usually brought back booty to be stored in the temple of their god, because their victory was understood as the defeat of one god by another (v.5). The Philistines took the Ark of the Covenant to the temple of Dagon (1 Sam 5:2) and, later, the armor of King Saul to the temple of Ashtaroth (1 Sam 31:10). The Babylonian Exile had been interpreted by the victors as proof of the weakness of Yahweh. The Israelites had smarted under these taunts (Ps 44:13-16); Joel had been concerned that the locust invasion might be an occasion for more taunts (Joel 2:17).

PLOWSHARES INTO SWORDS
3:9-16 (4:9-16 NAB)

> ⁹Proclaim this among the nations:
> Prepare war,
>   stir up the mighty men.

Let all the men of war draw near,
let them come up.
[10]Beat your plowshares into swords,
and your pruning hooks into spears;
let the weak say, "I am a warrior."

[11]Hasten and come,
all you nations round about,
gather yourselves there.
Bring down thy warriors, O LORD.
[12]Let the nations bestir themselves,
and come up to the valley of Jehoshaphat;
for there I will sit to judge
all the nations round about.

[13]Put in the sickle,
for the harvest is ripe.
Go in, tread,
for the wine press is full.
The vats overflow,
for their wickedness is great.

[14]Multitudes, multitudes,
in the valley of decision!
For the day of the LORD is near
in the valley of decision.
[15]The sun and the moon are darkened,
and the stars withdraw their shining.

[16]And the LORD roars from Zion,
and utters his voice from Jerusalem,
and the heavens and the earth shake.
But the LORD is a refuge to his people,
a stronghold to the people of Israel.

The Valley of Jehoshaphat now becomes the scene of
the final war between Yahweh and his foes (v.9). He turns
the taunts on them now, warning that even the farm implements and the weakest citizens will be needed for this battle

(v.10). In urging them to beat plowshares into swords and pruning hooks into spears, he is using the reverse of the messianic image popularized by Isaiah (Isa 2:4) and Micah (Mic 4:3) to warn that the peace prophesied by the ancient prophets will not exist for them.

The angelic host will accompany the Lord as his heavenly army (v.11). Their mission of vengeance is described in harvest terms, a familiar biblical image (Isa 17:5-6; 24:13; 63:1-3; Mt 13:39-42; Rev 14:14-20). The grain and grape harvest in Palestine was followed by the winemaking. The overflowing vats (v.13) symbolize the enormous wickedness of Israel's enemies and the generous punishment (treading) they will receive, a contrast to the plentiful blessing for the children of Zion (2:24). By quoting the eighth century prophet, Amos—"The Lord roars from Zion" (v.16; Amos 1:2)—Joel subtly reminds his readers that his strictures on Israel's enemies are only an updating of earlier prophecy. The Lord's voice will make heaven and earth shake (see Hag 2:20). But Yahweh will not forget his own. His strength will be a source of confidence, not fear, for his people.

JERUSALEM SHALL BE HOLY
3:17-21 (4:17-21 NAB)

> [17]"So you shall know that I am the LORD your God,
>   who dwell in Zion, my holy mountain.
> And Jerusalem shall be holy
>   and strangers shall never again pass through it.
>
> [18]"And in that day
> the mountains shall drip sweet wine,
>   and the hills shall flow with milk,
> and all the stream beds of Judah
>   shall flow with water;
> and a fountain shall come forth from
>   the house of the LORD
> and water the valley of Shittim.

¹⁹"Egypt shall become a desolation
    and Edom a desolate wilderness,
for the violence done to the people of Judah,
    because they have shed innocent blood in their land.
²⁰But Judah shall be inhabited for ever,
    and Jerualem to all generations.
²¹I will avenge their blood, and I will not clear the guilty,
    for the LORD dwells in Zion."

What began as a cry of alarm now ends as a paean of praise and confidence. The locust invasion did not bring destruction and neither will Israel's hostile neighbors, if Yahweh's people continue to put their hope in him. His halting of the locust plague was a proof of his willingness to save and a sign of his future judgment and destruction of his (and their) enemies on the day of the Lord. The suffering of the Hebrews, especially the Exile, had called Yahweh's presence and power into question, but his rule will be established definitively at Jehoshaphat: "So you shall know that I am the Lord your God" (v.17).

Joel evokes the grandiose imagery of Amos 9:13 to picture the bounty of the messianic age—mountains dripping wine, hills flowing with milk (v.18)—but he is unable to speak in terms of wide-open universalism. During the monarchy the Hebrew nation was able to think of itself as on a par with other nations. Now batterings and beatings from far and near have reduced Judah to a small enclave of resistance. The nation has retrenched within a small compass, viewing the outside world as hostile and evil. The prophet is unable to portray the messianic age as a time when "All the nations shall flow toward Jerusalem" (Isa 2:2-4; Mic 4:1-3); salvation is only for the Hebrews: "Strangers shall never again pass through it" (v.17).

The narrowness reflected here falls far short of the reality of God's nature and his plan; Joel and his compatriots have strong faith, but it needs to be enlightened and expanded. This is a good example of the Lord's patient guidance of his people, accepting them as they are, affirming their good points but nudging them to a deeper penetration of the mystery of God and his people. As a record of this process, the books of the Bible do not stand by themselves, independent of one another. They are even more than a library, for they interact. Joel's deep faith and trust in Yahweh's power and redemptive presence is a needed contrast to Lamentations; Joel's restricted point of view receives a necessary corrective from the universalism of Jonah.

A Catholic who has lived through the time of Vatican Council II can project the kind of trauma and/or liberation Joel's contemporaries have in store for them. Before the Council Catholics had a good deal of the same kind of feeling of being under siege by a hostile world. The Church became a safe fortress. Inside was salvation. One had to come to the Church to find this salvation. There were strict rules to protect those within the Church from outside influences. Then came Vatican II with the proclamation of a message of universal salvation. This caused real bewilderment and suffering to many in the Church who perceived this as a sudden about-face. Those who had been prepared for it, however, experienced a "breath of fresh air," to paraphrase Pope John XXIII. The same liberating experience opened to others as they understood Vatican II's teaching as a faithful interpretation of God's saving plan.

In dry Palestine, plentiful water easily became an image of messianic blessings (v.18; Ezek 47:1-2; Zech 14:8; Jn 4:10-15). The Valley of Shittim mentioned here has not been identified. It is certainly not Shittim east of the Jordan (Num 25:1; Josh 2:1). The name, which means "Valley of the Acacias," may be symbolic or prophetic. The reference probably has been inspired by the Spring of Gihon which emanated from the hill on which the Temple was located. It may be the same as the Wadies-Sant which flows westward to the Mediterranean Sea. The stream described by Ezekiel flows eastward to the Dead Sea (Ezek 47:8). Second Zechariah, writing later, combines these two traditions: the water from the Temple flows both east and west (Zech 14:8).

In a last flourish, the prophet recalls again the fate of Israel's enemies because of their treatment of God's people. Egypt and Edom will be desolate wildernesses, but Judah "shall be inhabited for ever" (v.19). The final sentence sums up the message Joel wants to leave with his readers: do not fear locust plagues or other natural disasters, nor the enmity of your neighbors, for Yahweh is present in the midst of his people (v.21).

Bibliography

G. Denzer, *The Books of Haggai, Zechariah, Malachi, Joel*, pages 35-47.

S. R. Driver, *The Books of Joel and Amos* (Cambridge Bible for Schools and Colleges). Cambridge and New York: Cambridge University Press, 1915.

E. H. Maly, *Prophets of Salvation*. New York: Herder and Herder, 1967. Pages 179-85.

C. Moore, *Baruch* (Anchor Bible), Garden City: Doubleday.

F. R. Stephenson, "The Date of the Book of Joel," *VT* 19 (April, 1969), 224-229.

J. D. W. Watts, *The Books of Joel, Obadiah, Jonah, Nahum, Habbakuk and Zephaniah*.

H. W. Wolff, *Amos and Joel* (Hermeneia), Philadelphia: Fortress, 1972.

Second Zechariah

SECOND ZECHARIAH
(Zechariah 9-14)

Background

THE DECISION TO PLACE THIS PART of the Book of
Zechariah in its proper chronological sequence after the
Book of Joel has already been mentioned in the commentaries on Zechariah and Malachi. Between Chapters Eight
and Nine of Zechariah we move to a completely new arena
in the history of Israel, at least two hundred years later and
possibly more. Unlike Chapters One through Eight, in this
section there are no dates and no clear historical allusions.
There is no mention of the central figures of the earlier
chapters, Joshua and Zerubbabel, nor of the rebuilding
of the Temple, which focused so much of the prophecy
of Haggai and Zechariah. Though there are no dates given,
three features of these chapters are helpful in making an
educated guess about when they were compiled.

The first indication comes from internal arguments
based on the biblical literature itself. Second Zechariah,
besides ample use of pre-exilic and exilic prophecy (Hosea,
Isaiah, Jeremiah, Second Isaiah, Ezekiel), also occasionally
shows dependence on the prophecy of Joel. Zechariah 12
and 14 allude to the eschatological war in Jerusalem when
the hostile nations will come against Yahweh and his
people: a picture of the last age that originated in Joel 4.

There is also abundant mention of the "day of the Lord" as in Joel and use of the imagery of life-giving water flowing from the Jerusalem Temple (Zech 14:8; Joel 4:18; though both of these may be dependent separately on Ezek 47:1-12). The Book of Joel is dated to about 400 B.C. Second Zechariah would not be earlier than that. And it cannot be later than 200 B.C. if the Book of Sirach, composed at that time, is speaking of the "Twelve (minor) Prophets" (Sir 49:10), which includes the Book of Zechariah, as a completed section of the Bible.

Further help in pinpointing the historical context of the prophecy comes from detection of allusions to contemporary events. Most scholars now agree in finding references to the conquests of Alexander the Great after his victory over the Persians in 333 B.C. This will be explained more completely in Chapter Nine, where the description of Yahweh's march through Syria, Lebanon and Palestine parallels remarkably the path of Alexander. This evidence, coupled with the dependence on Joel, leads to the dating of Second Zechariah in the last quarter of the fourth century B.C. (c. 325). The third feature which confirms this dating is the apocalyptic style adopted in some of the oracles, especially Chapter Fourteen, a style which was coming into prominence in this period.

A Humble Messiah

There is still royal messianism in these chapters, and even mention of King David and his family, but it is not as sharp and convincing as in Zechariah 1-8, when a descendant of David was still ruling. Now the promise to David and to Jerusalem is incorporated into a broader concept of messianism and into the wider context of Judah. A significant difference in the concept of the Messiah is his association with the poor remnant of Israel, and the image of this figure as humble and peaceful instead of lordly and warlike (9:9-10).

The latter half of Zechariah has special significance for Christians, because these few chapters were a favorite source for New Testament writers in describing the saving work of Jesus. The Savior himself even consciously dramatized one of the scenes of Second Zechariah in making his triumphal entry into Jerusalem. The scene is described in all four Gospels; Matthew and John quote Zechariah explicitly (Zech 9:9; Mt 21:5; Jn 12:15). Matthew makes the connection between Judas' thirty pieces of silver (Mt 26:15; 27:3-10) and the wages of the shepherd (Zech 11:12-13); and alludes to the condition of the sheep without a shepherd (Zech 10:2; Mt 9:36). Both Matthew and John refer to the "Song of the Sword" (Zech 12:7-9) in noting the disappearance of the apostles at the arrest of Jesus (Mt 26:31; Jn 16:32; also Mk 14:27). The Johannine literature uses material about the worthless shepherd (Zech 11:17; Jn 10:12-13), the pierced figure (Zech 12:10; Jn 19:37; Rev 1:7), the fountain of lifegiving water (Zech 13:1; Jn 7:38; 19:34; Rev 22:1-2), and the continuous daylight of the eschatological kingdom (Zech 14:6-7; Rev 21:23). The description of the cleansing of the Temple, present in the Synoptics (Mt 21:12-13; Mk 11:15-17; Lk 19:45-46), is more affected by the idea of trading (Zech 14:12) in John's account (2:16).

Christian readers will find a rich spiritual experience in reading these chapters slowly, trying to put themselves in the shoes of the evangelists and other early believers in Jesus. Listen as they did for the echoes of Christian fulfillment in the specific passages mentioned above, and also in the overall themes of messianic fulfillment, universalism of salvation and worship, suffering as the way to glory, the establishment of a completely new order.

Place in the Canon

The introduction to Malachi discussed how Second Zechariah and Malachi came to be associated in the formation of the Hebrew Bible. To summarize briefly: there were three independent collections of prophetic material appended to the collection of eleven minor prophets; each of these was introduced by the title "An oracle." The first two collections became Zechariah 9-11 and Zechariah 12-14; the third became the Book of Malachi. The first two oracles became connected to Zechariah 1-8 rather than grouped with the third oracle (Malachi) probably because they share with Zechariah the theme of messianism. But the messianism of Zechariah 1-8 is national, even Davidic, while the messianism of Zechariah 9-14 is apocalyptic.

THE BEGINNING OF THE END
CHAPTERS 9-11

THE TITLE "AN ORACLE" appears twice in Second Zechariah, at the beginning of Chapters Nine and Twelve, effectively dividing the book into two parts. The whole book has to do with the establishment of the messianic reign; but Chapters 9-11 deal primarily with the inaugural activities (e.g., subjugation of foreign enemies, return of the exiles), while Chapters 12-14 speak of the final struggles and establishment of the universal kingdom. Zechariah 14 is a collection of several oracles with the most pronounced apocalyptic tone of the book.

There are no dates in the text of Second Zechariah, but several clues in Chapter Nine (as sketched briefly above) relate the oracle to the conquests of Alexander the Great. In 333 B.C. Alexander overcame Darius III and the Persians at the crucial battle of the Plain of Issus (in modern-day Turkey near the border with Syria). He then advanced southwards, capturing the fortress of Tyre on the Phoenician coast and Gaza before entering Egypt. The progress of the Lord's "invasion" of the land follows the conquering trail of Alexander. Though he is not mentioned, Alexander seems to be considered the instrument of the Lord like other non-Jewish forces before him: Assyria (Isa 10:5), Cyrus the Persian (Isa 45:1). Earlier, the disruption of the Persian Empire at the time of the accession of Darius I

(522 B.C.) had been interpreted as the "shaking of the nations" (Hag 1:7; 2:22); now the overthrow of the ruling Persians 200 years later is seen again as the beginning of the messianic age.

THE LORD'S VICTORIOUS PATH
9:1-8
An Oracle

9 The word of the LORD is against the land of Hadrach
and will rest upon Damascus.
For to the LORD belong the cities of Aram,
even as all the tribes of Israel;
²Hamath also, which borders thereon,
Tyre and Sidon, though they are very wise.
³Tyre has built herself a rampart,
and heaped up silver like dust,
and gold like the mud of the streets.
⁴But lo, the Lord will strip her of her possessions
and hurl her wealth into the sea,
and she shall be devoured by fire.
⁵Ashkelon shall see it, and be afraid;
Gaza too, and shall writhe in anguish;
Ekron also, because its hopes are confounded.
The king shall perish from Gaza;
Ashkelon shall be uninhabited;
⁶a mongrel people shall dwell in Ashdod;
and I will make an end of the pride of Philistia.
⁷I will take away its blood from its mouth,
and its abominations from between its teeth;
it too shall be a remnant for our God;
it shall be like a clan in Judah,
and Ekron shall be like the Jebusites.
⁸Then I will encamp at my house as a guard,
so that none shall march to and fro;
no oppressor shall again overrun them,
for now I see with my own eyes.

God's decree of judgment, his "word," is perceived as a substantial presence that sets up headquarters in Damascus (v.1) in the midst of the cities of Aram (Syria). Isaiah had described the word of judgment in similar terms which Father John L. McKenzie compared to a time-bomb: "The Lord has sent a word against Jacob, and it will light upon Israel" (Isa 9:8). God's word means his effective presence. These territories also belong to Yahweh and will be incorporated into his kingdom, even if they are proud of their wisdom and wealth like Tyre (Ezek 28:1-10), which though a strong maritime power succumbed to Alexander after a seven-month siege. This oracle, viewed here as applicable to the conquests of Alexander, is believed by some scholars to be an old prophecy from Assyrian times.

The purification is painted in violent terms. Tyre will be destroyed by fire (vv.3-4); the Philistine cities, traditional enemies of Israel, will "writhe in anguish" as their leaders and people are despoiled. Ashdod can look forward to being displaced to some extent by a "mongrel people" (v.6), just as the Israelites saw their land and institutions encroached upon by foreigners after the fall of Samaria (2 Kgs 17:24-33). The Philistine cities will have to adopt rules for Jewish ritual purity, symbolized here by the restriction on eating meat with the blood still in it (Lev 17:10-16). In primitive biology blood was the bearer of life; the Jews would not eat the "life" of an animal because it belonged to God.

Once they have been purified, even these hostile pagan peoples will be a "remnant" (v.7), part of the nucleus of the messianic people. They will be incorporated into Judah just as the Jebusites, the original Canaanite inhabitants of Jerusalem, were incorporated into Israel by King David (2 Sam 24:18-25). When the land has been established in its new composition, including Israel and her formerly hostile neighbors, Yahweh will make his definitive "encampment" there to protect it from further harm (v.8).

YOUR KING COMES
9:9-13

⁹Rejoice greatly, O daughter of Zion!
   Shout aloud, O daughter of Jerusalem!
Lo, your king comes to you;
   triumphant and victorious is he,
humble and riding on an ass,
   on a colt the foal of an ass.
¹⁰I will cut off the chariot from Ephraim
   and the war horse from Jerusalem;
and the battle bow shall be cut off,
   and he shall command peace to the nations;
his dominion shall be from sea to sea,
   and from the River to the ends of the earth.
¹¹As for you also, because of the blood
   of my covenant with you,
I will set your captives free from the waterless pit.
¹²Return to your stronghold, O prisoners of hope;
   today I declare that I will restore to you double.
¹³For I have bent Judah as my bow;
   I have made Ephraim its arrow.
I will brandish your sons, O Zion,
   over your sons, O Greece,
      and wield you like a warrior's sword.

Suddenly there is heightened excitement as Jerusalem
is roused to attention: "Rejoice greatly, O daughter of
Zion!" Such outbursts of joy at the presence of the Lord
in the midst of his people after a time of bitter suffering
were familiar from exilic prophecies: "Shout, O Israel! . . .
The Lord; your God is in your midst"(Zeph 3:14,17); "Sing,
O Heavens, for the Lord has done it; shout, O depths of the
earth" (Isa 44:23). The optimism of Second Isaiah was occasioned by the victories of Cyrus the Persian which
paralleled the exultant spirit of Second Zechariah at the
progress of Alexander the Great. Exultation greets the

advent of the king, a theme familiar from the psalms (Pss 81:2; 95:1-2; 97:1).

But there is something startling about the description of the king, "triumphant and victorious" but "humble and riding on an ass" (v.9). The text rings familiar to Christian ears because of its use in the New Testament to interpret Jesus' entry into Jerusalem: "Tell the daughter of Zion, Behold, your king is coming to you, humble and mounted on an ass, and on a colt, the foal of an ass" (Mt 21:5; see Jn 12:15). The emphasis is not on humility so much as on peaceful intent. Riding on an ass was not demeaning to the princes of old: Judah (Gen 49:10-11); the judges (Judg 5:10; 12:14); David and Solomon (1 Kgs 1:33). When the king came as a warrior, though, he rode a horse (Jer 8:6; Nah 3:2-3). The description of the king should be "just and saved" rather than "triumphant and victorious." The Greek translators had a difficult time accepting the messianic ruler as "saved," and read the description as "just savior" (NAB). But the king here is "just and saved"; the emphasis is on the king as the head of his people. He leads them in justice and salvation.

The messianic king will inaugurate a season of peace (v.10). Not only will the northern kingdom (Ephraim) and the southern kingdom (Jerusalem) lay down their weapons and cease hostilities with foreigners and with one another, but peace will encompass the whole world: from the Mediterranean Sea to the Persian Gulf, from the Euphrates River to the uncharted "ends of the earth." In spite of passages like this one, proclaiming the peaceful rule of an unwarlike king or the leader as servant of the people (Isa 52 - 53), the popular tradition continued to paint a military image of the coming Messiah.

These verses are a witness to the tenacious hope instilled in Israel by the promise to David (2 Sam 7). The Davidic dynasty had seemed to end with the Exile, then flickered briefly again in Zerubbabel before finally being snuffed out. There had been no king for two hundred years, but the hope in a Davidic Messiah remains strong. Adversity, as always, has purified and interiorized this hope. The fading of kingly glory in Israel permitted the idea of the humble, peaceful leader to emerge; this seems to be a blending with the post-exilic theme of the poor and lowly remnant, the *anawim*, who would serve as the nucleus of the restored nation. The fall of Israel had come about because of the wicked oppression of the rich; its restoration will depend on the "poor of Yahweh," who because of their own emptiness are able to let the Lord work in their midst according to his ancient design. "Blessed are the poor in spirit" (Mt 5:3).

HOW GOOD IT SHALL BE!
9:14-17

> ¹⁴Then the LORD will appear over them,
>   and his arrow go forth like lightning;
> the Lord GOD will sound the trumpet,
>   and march forth in the whirlwinds of the south.
> ¹⁵The LORD of hosts will protect them,
>   and they shall devour and tread down the slingers;
> and they shall drink their blood like wine,
>   and be full like a bowl,
>   drenched like the corners of the altar.
> ¹⁶On that day the LORD their God will save them
>   for they are the flock of his people;
> for like the jewels of a crown
>   they shall shine on his land.
> ¹⁷Yea, how good and how fair it shall be!
>   Grain shall make the young men flourish,
>   and new wine the maidens.

Though the Lord's anointed is described as peaceful (vv.9-10), the Lord himself is still pictured as a warrior (v.14). Psalm 18 is similar:

"He sent out his arrows, and scattered them;
he flashed forth lightnings, and routed them" (v.14).

The cosmic battle will be won for the people of God at the cost of much bloodshed among their enemies (v.15). Enemy blood on the Israelite warriors is connected with the sacrificial blood sprinkled on the altar (Lev 1:5). This is an oblique reference to the covenant and to God's covenant fidelity in protecting Israel in the eschatological struggle. Moses sprinkled blood over altar and people to symbolize Yahweh's union with his people (Ex 24:6-8). In this vision the altar and the people are one (v.15).

After the slaughter, the day of the Lord dawns over Israel. The people, jewels in God's crown, shine like the dawn themselves (v.16). There will be peace and abundance of blessings on that day. The emblems of agricultural prosperity are abundance of grain and wine (Ps 4:8). The flock of the Lord will be well pastured (v.17).

SHEEP WITHOUT A SHEPHERD
10:1-5

10 Ask rain from the LORD
   in the season of the spring rain,
from the LORD who makes the storm clouds,
   who gives men showers of rain,
   to every one the vegetation in the field.
²For the teraphim utter nonsense,
   and the diviners see lies;
the dreamers tell false dreams,
   and give empty consolation.
Therefore the people wander like sheep;
   they are afflicted for want of a shepherd.

³"My anger is hot against the shepherds,
   and I will punish the leaders;
for the LORD of hosts cares for his
   flock, the house of Judah,
and will make them like his proud
   steed in battle.
⁴Out of them shall come the cornerstone,
   out of them the tent peg,

out of them the battle bow,
out of them every ruler.
⁵Together they shall be like mighty men in battle,
trampling the foe in the mud of the streets;
they shall fight because the LORD is with them,
and they shall confound the riders on horses.

The theme of divine victory and restoration of the people continues in this chapter. Israel has come to realize that Yahweh is the Lord of nature; his guidance of the seasons does not depend on spring fertility rites. Neither does it make any sense to consult teraphim (household idols used for divination) or fortune tellers (v.2). The people have been reduced to this because of false leaders, but the Lord himself will be their shepherd now.

The image of God's people as sheep without a shepherd, wandering aimlessly and falling into sin, is a traditional one in Israel (Num 27:17; 1 Kgs 22:17). Ezekiel developed this picture into a lengthy accusation of the pre-exilic leaders (Ezek 34:1-10). In days to come, though, Yahweh himself will be the shepherd: "I will seek the lost, and I will bring back the strayed, and I will bind up the crippled, and I will strengthen the weak, and the fat and the strong I will watch over; I will feed them in justice" (Ezek 34:16). The shepherd theme will be taken up again for the allegory of Zechariah 11.

In the new age leaders will be drawn from Israel who will be strong and firm, as symbolized by the cornerstone, the tent peg and the battle bow (v.4). They will prevail because "the Lord is with them" (v.5).

THE INGATHERING
10:6 - 11:3

⁶"I will strengthen the house of Judah,
and I will save the house of Joseph.
I will bring them back because I have
compassion on them,

and they shall be as though I had not rejected them;
   for I am the LORD their God and I will answer them.
⁷Then Ephraim shall become like a mighty warrior,
   and their hearts shall be glad as with wine.
Their children shall see it and rejoice,
   their hearts shall exult in the LORD.

⁸"I will signal for them and gather them in,
   for I have redeemed them,
   and they shall be as many as of old.
⁹Though I scattered them among the nations,
   yet in far countries they shall remember me,
   and with their children they shall live and return.
¹⁰I will bring them home from the land of Egypt,
   and gather them from Assyria;
and I will bring them to the land of Gilead and to
      Lebanon,
   till there is no room for them.

¹¹They shall pass through the sea of Egypt,
   and the waves of the sea shall be smitten,
   and all the depths of the Nile dried up.
The pride of Assyria shall be laid low,
   and the scepter of Egypt shall depart.
¹²I will make them strong in the LORD
   and they shall glory in his name,"
                                        says the LORD.

11 Open your doors, O Lebanon,
   that the fire may devour your cedars!
²Wail, O cypress, for the cedar has fallen,
   for the glorious trees are ruined!
Wail, oaks of Bashan,
   for the thick forest has been felled!
³Hark, the wail of the shepherds,
   for their glory is despoiled!
Hark, the roar of the lions,
   for the jungle of the Jordan is laid waste!

The author uses the well-known events of Israel's past to make vivid God's message of restoration to his contemporaries. We read of scattering and gathering, of Egypt and Assyria, though the author is describing an interior transformation. The imagery of these events (as of later salvation events in Jesus) interpret for us today our own particular experience of suffering and restoration.

The restoration in the new age will be larger than the territory of Judah, which has formed the core of the new "holy land" since the time of the Exile. There is a refreshing breadth of view in the inclusion of the old northern kingdom (represented by "Joseph" and "Ephraim": vv.6-7), which at this time is occupied by the distrusted Samaritans. Ephraim will even receive its former place of greatness as a mighty warrior (Judg 7:24-25; 8:1-3; Ps 60:9).

The Lord will call his people home (v.8). The verb translated as "signal" (*sharaq*) is more accurately rendered "whistle" (JB, NAB, NEB), "hiss" (KJ) or "pipe." This is the reverse of the Lord's whistling to the "fly" of Egypt and the "bee" of Assyria to carry the people away (Isa 7:18; see 5:26-30). The description of the return brings Hosea's beautiful language to mind:

"They shall come trembling like birds from Egypt,
    and like doves from the land of Assyria;
    and I will return them to their homes,
    says the Lord" (Hos 11:11).

The people will begin to resettle in the places first invaded from the north: Gilead in Transjordan (2 Kgs 15:29) and Lebanon, which had been the upper extremity of David's kingdom (2 Sam 8:6). When Israel is filled to its ancient borders still more room will be needed (v.10). The return will be so vast it will seem like a repeat of the Exodus (v.11).

The first three verses of Chapter Eleven conclude this section describing the victorious return of God's people and the overthrow of Israel's enemies. They form a taunt-song in which the foreign rulers who have oppressed Israel are compared to trees of the forest. Isaiah had used this image in taunting Assyria (Isa 10:33-34), Ezekiel in taunting Egypt (Ezek 31). The nations are caught in a disastrous forest fire, and their leaders (shepherds, lions) are trapped. All is clear for a new beginning in the glorious reign of Yahweh.

THE ALLEGORY OF THE SHEPHERDS
11:4-17

⁴Thus said the LORD my God: "Become shepherd of the flock doomed to slaughter. ⁵Those who buy them slay them and go unpunished; and those who sell them say, 'Blessed be the LORD, I have become rich'; and their own shepherds have no pity on them. ⁶For I will no longer have pity on the inhabitants of this land, says the LORD. Lo, I will cause men to fall each into the hand of his shepherd, and each into the hand of his king; and they shall crush the earth, and I will deliver none from their hand."

⁷So I became the shepherd of the flock doomed to be slain for those who trafficked in the sheep. And I took two staffs; one I named Grace, the other I named Union. And I tended the sheep. ⁸In one month I destroyed the three shepherds. But I became impatient with them, and they also detested me. ⁹So I said, "I will not be your shepherd. What is to die, let it die; what is to be destroyed, let it be destroyed; and let those that are left devour the flesh of one another." ¹⁰And I took my staff Grace, and I broke it, annulling the covenant which I had made with all the peoples. ¹¹So it was annulled on that day, and the traffickers in the sheep, who were watching me, knew that it was the word of the LORD. ¹²Then I said to them, "If it seems right to you, give me my wages; but if not, keep them." And they weighed out as my wages thirty shekels of silver. ¹³Then the LORD said to me, "Cast it into the treasury"—the lordly price at which I was paid

off by them. So I took the thirty shekels of silver and cast them into the treasury in the house of the LORD. [14]Then I broke my second staff Union, annulling the brotherhood between Judah and Israel.

[15]Then the LORD said to me, "Take once more the implements of a worthless shepherd. [16]For lo, I am raising up in the land a shepherd who does not care for the perishing, or seek the wandering, or heal the maimed, or nourish the sound, but devours the flesh of the fat ones, tearing off even their hoofs.

[17]Woe to my worthless shepherd,
who deserts the flock!
May the sword smite his arm
and his right eye!
Let his arm be wholly withered,
his right eye utterly blinded!"

The allegory of the shepherds harks back again to the time of persecution, as before envisioning these difficulties as an opportunity for purification before the inauguration of the messianic era. The prophet is called by God to shepherd the people, because the foreign rulers have abused them, and "their own shepherds" (v.5) are no better. The prophet symbolically takes two staffs for his mission as shepherd, naming them Grace (or Favor: NAB) and Union (or Bonds). Grace stands for God's covenant with his people; Union for the bonding of the northern and southern kingdoms of Israel and Judah after pre-exilic generations of separation.

The three shepherds destroyed by the prophet (v.8) have not been successfully identified. They may have been high priests or leaders of Jerusalem factions in the prophet's own day. The prophet himself is then rejected by the people, probably because he makes moral demands in preparing them for the messianic age. He breaks Grace, annulling the covenant, and Union, breaking Israel in two again (vv.10,14). The breaking of Union most likely refers to the final rupture between Judah and Samaria in about 328 B.C. (shortly before the composition of Second Zechariah) when, according to the Jewish historian Josephus, the Samaritans built their own temple on Mount Gerizim in opposition to the Jerusalem Temple.

The people respond quickly to the request for wages for the good shepherd, so happy are they to get rid of him (v.12). But the price they give is a slap in the face, thirty shekels of silver, the indemnity for a gored slave (Ex 21:32), a sum familiar to Christians as the amount paid Judas for his treason (Mt 26:15). The money is thrown into the Temple treasury, for in rejecting the prophet the people have really been rejecting Yahweh (Mt 27:3-6). The word "treasury"(v.13) is an emendation of the Hebrew text, which reads "potter." Interestingly, both readings are reflected in the story of Judas in Matthew's Gospel (Mt 27:5,7). In the place of the good shepherd, the Lord raised up a worthless shepherd who will punish the people (v.16). The people will suffer, but so will this worthless shepherd (v.17).

MESSIANIC JERUSALEM
CHAPTERS 12-14

JUDAH AND JERUSALEM
12:1-9

An Oracle

12 The word of the LORD concerning Israel: Thus says the LORD, who stretched out the heavens and founded the earth and formed the spirit of man within him: ²"Lo, I am about to make Jerusalem a cup of reeling to all the peoples round about; it will be against Judah also in the siege against Jerusalem. ³On that day I will make Jerusalem a heavy stone for all the peoples; all who lift it shall grievously hurt themselves. And all the nations of the earth will come together against it. ⁴On that day, says the LORD, I will strike every horse with panic, and its rider with madness. But upon the house of Judah I will open my eyes, when I strike every horse of the peoples with blindness. ⁵Then the clans of Judah shall say to themselves, 'The inhabitants of Jerusalem have strength through the LORD of hosts, their God.'

⁶"On that day I will make the clans of Judah like a blazing pot in the midst of wood, like a flaming torch among sheaves; and they shall devour to the right and to the left all the peoples round about, while Jerusalem shall still be inhabited in its place, in Jerusalem.

⁷"And the LORD will give victory to the tents of Judah first, that the glory of the house of David and the glory of the inhabitants of Jerusalem may not be exalted over that of Judah. ⁸On that day the LORD will put a shield about the inhabitants of Jerusalem so that the feeblest among them on that day shall be like David, and the house of David shall be like God, like the angel of the LORD, at their head. ⁹And on that day I will seek to destroy all the nations that come against Jerusalem.

The title, "An Oracle," indicates that the final three chapters are separate from what went before. The chapters are also of a later vintage than the preceding, though they cannot date after 200 B.C. because Jesus ben Sira, author of Sirach (c. 180 B.C.), mentions "the twelve minor prophets" (Sir 49:10) as a complete section including these chapters. The new beginning is also suggested by the dramatic "The word of the Lord. . ." and "Thus says the Lord. . ." and by the majestic description of Yahweh as creator of the universe and mankind (v.1). There is also a more apocalyptic tone in these chapters, and the eschatological aspect of the messianic age is stressed. The expression "on that day," used several times in this chapter (vv.3,4,6,8,9,11), is the typical post-exilic announcement of final judgment and victory (see Joel 2:1-2).

Jerusalem is described as Yahweh's instrument in the punishment of the nations on the final day of vengeance. She is portrayed as a cup of God's wrath which will make her enemies drunk and vulnerable (v.2). This imagery for God's anger is typical of the prophets (Isa 51:17; Jer 25:15-16; Ezek 23:31-34). Various references about Judah's participation with Jerusalem in this climactic event (vv.2,5) and the equality of the surrounding country to the city (v.7) may be an echo of a quarrel some of the smaller towns had with the superiority complex of Jerusalemites. Jerusalem is compared to a stone that may lacerate those who try to move it (v.3; see Isa 8:14-15; 1 Pet 2:8).

The might of Jerusalem's enemies, represented by cavalry, is routed and thrown into panic as the Lord defends his people (v.4). The images of Judah as a blazing pot and a flaming torch are meant to emphasize the speed and thoroughness of the divine destruction of the enemies (v.6). The references to David and his "house" (vv.7-8) come at a time when his dynasty is at an all-time low (as in Chapter Nine) and show that hope in this promise still smolders in the hearts of the people. All the people of God will become like David, even the weakest (v.8).

THE ONE WHO WAS PIERCED
12:10 - 13:1

> [10]"And I will pour out on the house of David and the inhabitants of Jerusalem a spirit of compassion and supplication, so that, when they look on him whom they have pierced, they shall mourn for him, as one mourns for an only child, and weep bitterly over him, as one weeps over a first-born. [11]On that day the mourning in Jerusalem will be as great as the mourning for Hadad-rimmon in the plain of Megiddo. [12]The land shall mourn, each family by itself; the family of the house of David by itself, and their wives by themselves; the family of the house of Nathan by itself, and their wives by themselves; [13]the family of the house of Levi by itself, and their wives by themselves; the family of the Shimeites by itself, and their wives by themselves; [14]and all the families that are left, each by itself, and their wives by themselves.
> **13** "On that day there shall be a fountain opened for the house of David and the inhabitants of Jerusalem to cleanse them from sin and uncleanness."

There is a sudden shift of mood to lamentation as we come on verse 10, another one of the most enigmatic and most discussed verses in Second Zechariah. Several themes of Hebrew history and prophecy crisscross in verses 10-11, with a further depth involved by the implications this text has for the interpretation of Jesus' role in the New Testament. The mention of pouring out the spirit connects us to the promise of restoration of the nation in Ezekiel (36:26-27; 37:5-14; 39:29), the description of the onset of the messianic age in Joel (2:28-29) which is later used by St. Peter to interpret the effects of the gift of the Spirit in the early Christian community (Acts 2:17-21), the description of the spirit-filled Davidic Messiah of Isaiah (11:1-3), and of the Suffering Servant of Second Isaiah (Isa 42:1-4; see 61:1-4).

The people of Jerusalem are given a spirit of "compassion" (or better, "grace": NAB) by which they are able to be pleasing to God, and a spirit of "supplication" which helps them request divine mercy. The person "whom they have pierced" has tantalized commentators through the centuries. Is this a reference to a contemporary figure, perhaps a charismatic prophet cast out by the official leaders (maybe even, if the two texts are not too separated by time, the "good shepherd" mentioned in Chapter Eleven)? St. John sees this as a prophecy fulfilled in the death of Jesus on the cross (Jn 19:37); the Book of Revelation, which in various ways presents the glorified Jesus still exhibiting the marks of his wounds, uses this text in a future sense of the last judgment (Rev 1:7). The mention of "an only child" further enhanced the interpretation of this mysterious figure as a type or foreshadowing of Jesus (Jn 3:16).

Hadad-rimmon and Megiddo call attention to two examples of mourning, one pagan, the other Hebrew (v.11). Hadad and Rimmon were pagan weather gods, Hadad a god of storms, Rimmon a god of the seasons worshiped in Damascus. The beginning of winter was associated with the death of Rimmon, spring with his rebirth; each fall there were rites of mourning. The mention of Megiddo in connection with bitter mourning recalls the death of the beloved king Josiah in a battle at Megiddo in 609 B.C. According to the Chronicler, this loss was commemorated in regular national rites of lamentation (2 Chr 35:24-25).

The mourning for "him whom they have pierced" is spelled out at great length. It will involve the royal family (identified by David and Nathan) and the priestly family (Levi and the Shimeites; see Num 3:18), in fact all the families of Israel (vv.12-14). The notation concerning the "wives by themselves" refers to the practice of separation of men and women in liturgy which is still observed among the Jews. There is a well-known textual problem in verse 10. The Hebrew text, followed by most ancient versions, reads "they look on *me* whom they have pierced." The idea of Yahweh's being "pierced" causes problems. Some versions found different interpretations for the Hebrew word for "pierce" (*daqar*): the Greek translation reads "insulted." The one "whom they have pierced," at any rate, remains a thorny question of identification. It can hardly be Yahweh. Is it the prophetic shepherd of 11:7? Perhaps the shepherd symbolizes all the suffering prophets of Israel, "pierced" by the hardhearted people.

Verse one of Chapter Thirteen was mistakenly separated from the foregoing. The mourning caused by the tragedy recounted in the preceding verses prepared the people for the cleansing waters that will wash away their sin and uncleanness. Ezekiel described a vision of life-giving water flowing from the Temple of the messianic age (Ezek 47:1-12). Jesus is portrayed as the source of the true life-giving water (the Holy Spirit) in the Gospel of John (Jn 4:10-15; 7:37-39). The image is applied to the Lamb and the heavenly city in Revelation: ". . . the river of the water of life, bright as crystal, flowing from the throne of God and of the Lamb through the middle of the street of the city" (Rev 22:1-2; 7:17).

DOWN WITH PROPHETS
13:2-6

[2]"And on that day, says the LORD of hosts, I will cut off the names of the idols from the land, so that they

shall be remembered no more; and also I will remove
from the land the prophets and the unclean spirit. ³And
if any one again appears as a prophet, his father and
mother who bore him will say to him, 'You shall not live,
for you speak lies in the name of the LORD'; and his
father and mother who bore him shall pierce him through
when he prophesies. ⁴On that day every prophet will be
ashamed of his vision when he prophesies; he will not put
on a hairy mantle in order to deceive, ⁵but he will say,
'I am no prophet, I am a tiller of the soil; for the land
has been my possession since my youth.' ⁶And if one asks
him, 'What are these wounds on your back?' he will say,
'The wounds I received in the house of my friends.'"

With verse 2, Chapter Thirteen returns to the familiar
process of punishment - repentance - restoration. The
national sinfulness is associated here primarily with false
prophecy. The role of the prophet is presented in very
pessimistic tones. Several of the prophets had spoken
critically of false prophets (Jer 23:9-32; Ezek 13:1-16), but
they had always held their own vocation in high esteem. The
writer does not distinguish in his harsh denunciation.
Perhaps the decline of prophecy by this time was understood as a judgment on "official" prophecy, the function
of advisors to the ruler.

Israel had traditionally recognized the possibility of
misleading and misled prophecy and been aware of the
difficulty of discerning true from false prophecy. A procedure for dealing with the false prophet (associated, as in
this chapter, with idolatry) is given in the book of Deuteronomy (13:1-9; 18:19-22). The punishment is to begin
at home, within the family. This is probably why the false
prophet's parents are mentioned in verse 3.

On the day of Yahweh, in the face of divine judgment,
the prophet will be so fearful of condemnation that he will
hide the mantle (v.4) that is the customary mark of his
profession (2 Kgs 1:8; Mt 3:4). He will mimic the words of

Amos as an escape (v.5: Amos 7:14). The scars of lacerations (v.6) he has received in idolatrous ritual (1 Kgs 18:28) will be passed off as wounds received in a neighborhood brawl. The disowning of the prophets in this chapter is alarming, a reminder that even the most sacred of vocations and institutions can be abused and fall into decline, and even be superseded. At the time this chapter was composed, the priests were the pillars of God's community, holding all together in the absence of kings and prophets. But the priests, too, were subject to decline and abuse, as we learn in documents from earlier and later times (for example, Mal 1:6-10; 2:1-9; Neh 13:29; Jn 11:47-53).

THE SONG OF THE SWORD
13:7-9

> [7]"Awake, O sword, against my shepherd,
>   against the man who stands next to me,"
>   says the LORD of hosts.
> "Strike the shepherd, that the sheep may be scattered;
> I will turn my hand against the little ones.
> [8]In the whole land, says the LORD,
>   two thirds shall be cut off and perish,
>   and one third shall be left alive.
> [9]And I will put this third into the fire,
>   and refine them as one refines silver,
>   and test them as gold is tested.
> They will call on my name,
>   and I will answer them.
> I will say, 'They are my people';
>   and they will say, 'The LORD is my God.'"

In this, another psalm about the "birthpangs of the Messiah," God's sword of punishment is commanded to strike (v.7). On another occasion, in a time of suffering, the sword was told to desist (Jer 47:6). The context is not the same as the shepherd passage in Chapter Eleven. There the shepherds were remiss in their duties: they were guilty. This shepherd is not condemned. He is even the Lord's associate, the "man who stands next to me." Why would Yahweh want to strike this shepherd of his people?

It is for the correction and purification of the sheep rather than the shepherd this time. Only one-third (a remnant) of them will pass the test (v.8). The Gospels use this text as a means of profound insight into the mystery of redemptive suffering in Christ. The "refining" of the Passion affects the flock through the shepherd, first negatively, then "super-positively" in the resurrection which emerges from the suffering. In the resurrection Jesus and his followers are enveloped by the glory of the Father (Mk 14:27; Mt 26:31). This makes for the richness of the New Testament fulfillment of the traditional covenant formula: "They are my people . . . . The Lord is my God" (Hos 2:23).

THE BATTLE FOR JERUSALEM
14:1-15

> **14** Behold, a day of the LORD is coming, when the spoil taken from you will be divided in the midst of you. ²For I will gather all the nations against Jerusalem to battle, and the city shall be taken and the houses plundered and the women ravished; half of the city shall go into exile, but the rest of the people shall not be cut off from the city. ³Then the LORD will go forth and fight against those nations as when he fights on a day of battle. ⁴On that day his feet shall stand on the Mount of Olives which lies before Jerusalem on the east; and the Mount of Olives shall be split in two from east to west by a very wide valley; so that one half of the Mount shall withdraw northward, and the other half southward. ⁵And the valley of my mountains shall be stopped up, for the valley of the mountains shall touch the side of it; and you shall flee as you fled from the earthquake in the days of Uzziah king of Judah. Then the LORD your God will come, and all the holy ones with him.

⁶On that day there shall be neither cold nor frost. ⁷And there shall be continuous day (it is known to the LORD), not day and not night, for at evening time there shall be light.

⁸On that day living waters shall flow out from Jerusalem, half of them to the eastern sea and half of them to the western sea; it shall continue in summer as in winter.

⁹And the LORD will become king over all the earth; on that day the LORD will be one and his name one.

¹⁰The whole land shall be turned into a plain from Geba to Rimmon south of Jerusalem. But Jerusalem shall remain aloft upon its site from the Gate of Benjamin to the place of the former gate, to the Corner Gate, and from the Tower of Hananel to the king's wine presses. ¹¹And it shall be inhabited, for there shall be no more curse; Jerusalem shall dwell in security.

¹²And this shall be the plague with which the LORD will smite all the peoples that wage war against Jerusalem: their flesh shall rot while they are still on their feet, their eyes shall rot in their sockets, and their tongues shall rot in their mouths. ¹³And on that day a great panic from the LORD shall fall on them, so that each will lay hold on the hand of his fellow, and the hand of the one will be raised against the hand of the other; ¹⁴even Judah will fight against Jerusalem. And the wealth of all the nations round about shall be collected, gold, silver, and garments in great abundance. ¹⁵And a plague like this plague shall fall on the horses, the mules, the camels, the asses, and whatever beasts may be in those camps.

The apocalyptic style reflected at various places in Second Zechariah reaches its zenith in this concluding chapter, the latest part of the book to be composed before the book was edited as a whole. Its characteristic coloring is noticed, for example, in verse 12's exaggerated description of the punishment of Jerusalem's enemies (see Ezek 39:17-20; Rev 19:17-18). In the familiar opening scenario, Jerusalem is besieged by her enemies. The city survives, but only after considerable suffering and destruction (v.2). Then Yahweh appears on the scene, coming from the sunrise like a rescuing charge of cavalry. The Mount of Olives and the Kidron Valley formed natural defensive barriers for Jerusalem on the east; in the face of the Lord's approach, the Mount of Olives will split in two and the valley will be filled in to form an east-west highway (vv.4-5; see Isa 40:3-5). The enemies of the Lord ("you" in v.5), seeing in this rearrangement of topography the definitive cataclysm, will flee as from the earthquake in the days of King Uzziah (750 B.C.; see Amos 1:1).

Ideal climate and living conditions always appear in the vision of the day of salvation: eternal light and warmth (Isa 60:19-20; Rev 21:23; 22:5); abundant waters (Ezek 47:1-12; Joel 4:18; Rev 22:1-2). The waters will be so plentiful they will flow both east (to the Dead Sea) and west (to the Mediterranean). Water supply is of immense importance in the dry climate of the Near East. Part of God's curse against Jerusalem's enemies is the withholding of needed rainfall (v.17); for Egypt, it will be a plague affecting the waters of the Nile (v.18).

In the messianic age, Yahweh will be the king of all, the only God of all the world (v.9). He will rule in Jerusalem, whose glory will be enhanced because all the surrounding hills will fall to the level of the plain "from Geba to Rimmon" (the northern and southern boundaries of Judah). Jerusalem, however, will remain aloft (v.10). The various locations indicate dimensions of the city: Gate of Benjamin to the Corner Gate = eastern and western boundaries; Tower of Hananel to the king's wine presses = northern and southern boundaries. It will be safe to dwell in Jerusalem because there will be no danger of the *herem* (v.11), the curse that decrees utter destruction (Josh 6:21). In verse 14, "Judah will fight *against* Jerusalem" is better translated "Judah will fight *with* (or in) Jerusalem."

THE ULTIMATE FESTIVAL
14:16-21

[16]Then every one that survives of all the nations that have come against Jerusalem shall go up year after year to worship the King, the LORD of hosts, and to keep the feast of booths. [17]And if any of the families of the earth do not go up to Jerusalem to worship the King, the LORD of hosts, there will be no rain upon them. [18]And if the family of Egypt do not go up and present themselves, then upon them shall come the plague with which the LORD afflicts the nations that do not go up to keep the feast of booths. [19]This shall be the punishment to Egypt and the punishment to all the nations that do not go up to keep the feast of booths.

[20]And on that day there shall be inscribed on the bells of the horses, "Holy to the LORD." And the pots in the house of the LORD shall be as the bowls before the altar; [21]and every pot in Jerusalem and Judah shall be sacred to the LORD of hosts, so that all who sacrifice may come and take of them and boil the flesh of the sacrifice in them. And there shall no longer be a trader in the house of the LORD of hosts on that day.

In the commentary of Haggai (2:1-9) it was noted that the universal pilgrimage to Jerusalem at the Feast of Booths, the fall festival of Tishri, the seventh month (September-October), had become a standard image of the messianic kingdom (Isa 2:2-4). The feast had originally celebrated God's care for his nomad people in the wilderness (Lev 23:43), but it had accumulated other memories of God's act of protection, and very importantly for the returning exiles, it had been the occasion for the dedication of Solomon's Temple (1 Kgs 8:2). In the messianic kingdom, presence at this feast will be a test of loyalty to Yahweh (vv.16-19). The eschatological symbol of the abundance of water is echoed here, too: this feast came just before the autumn rains and was an occasion for petitions for rain. The Talmud records the pouring of water at this feast. In John's Gospel, it is at the Feast of Booths that Jesus reveals himself as the source of the true living waters (Jn 7:37-39).

Horses were usually bearers of warlike invaders and the bells on their harnesses were superstitious charms. In the new age, horses will bring pilgrims to Jerusalem; the inscription on their bells will be the same as the inscription on the turbans of the high priests (v.20: Ex 28:36-38). There will be so many pilgrims that the sacred libation bowls, from which the blood of sacrificial animals was poured on the altar holocausts, will be insufficient to provide for the many sacrifices (vv.20-21). Household utensils will be converted to this use.

The final acerbic verse seems out of context in the glorious passage it concludes. There will no longer be "a trader" (literally, a "Canaanite") in the Temple (v.21). This may be a slap at the tendency to commercialism by the priests and other ministers in charge. The feast will be really glorious, comes the wry comment, when no one in the worshiping community is bending the celebration to his own benefit. Then God's people will really be at one.

Bibliography

G. Denzer, *The Books of Haggai, Zechariah, Malachi, Joel*, pages 48-62.

F. McDonagh, B. Robinson, and H. Swanstrom, *Prophets II*, pages 143-147.

W. Neil, "Book of Zechariah," *Interpreter's Bible*, Volume 4, pages 945-947.

D. S. Russell, *The Jews from Alexander to Herod*. London: Oxford University Press, 1967. Pages 200-212.

Baruch

BARUCH

Background

THE BOOK OF BARUCH is last in chronological sequence among the books under study in this volume. Though it is associated with the name of Jeremiah's secretary (Jer 32:12) and with the Babylonian Exile (587-538 B.C.), the book belongs to a much later time: the common view is that its various parts were written between the early second century and the mid-first century B.C., and that the book was edited in its present form around 50 B.C. Some of its admonitions concerning attitudes toward foreign rulers may have been tailored to reflect the situation in Palestine following the Roman occupation under Pompey in 63 B.C.

Baruch is an artificial unity of separate writings by different authors, compiled as a call for return to the sources of Hebrew faith at a time of complacency or loss of identity. It contains beautiful prayers based on biblical history and designed for use in synagogue worship. Though the book is extant only in Greek, at least part of it was originally in Hebrew. Baruch is one of the seven books of the Old Testament (along with Tobit, Judith, Wisdom, Sirach, 1 and 2 Maccabees) not accepted as inspired Scripture by Jews and Protestants. Bibles published for use by both Catholics and Protestants will include Baruch and the other disputed books in a section called "Apocrypha."

There are four clearly discernible sections in the Book of Baruch, two prose (first and fourth) and two poetry (middle sections):

1) 1:1—3:8: The prayer of the Hebrew exiles, preceded by an introduction setting the historical context.

2) 3:9—4:4: A hymn in praise of wisdom.

3) 4:5—5:9: Jerusalem consoling her children and receiving consolation.

4) 6:1-73: The Letter of Jeremiah to the exiles (originally published as a separate document independent of Baruch).

Various theories of dating have placed the final edition of the book as late as after 70 A.D. or as early as 180 B.C. The common view, adopted here, is based on conclusions about the relationship of parts of Baruch to other writings. Baruch 1:15—2:19 uses phrases and ideas similar to those in Daniel 9:7-19, which is dated to 164 B.C. For long it was held that Baruch borrowed from Daniel; now it seems more likely that they both depended on a common Jewish liturgical tradition. There are also parallels between Baruch 4:5—5:9 and Psalm 11 of the 18 Psalms of Solomon (a non-biblical collection compiled 60-30 B.C.). The view adopted here understands Baruch to have been used in the Psalm, but there are critics who see the dependence the other way.

The scene of the narrative is set in exilic Babylon where Baruch, the secretary of Jeremiah (who meanwhile has been deported to Egypt: Jer 44:1), is carrying on his master's work: gathering the exiles for the reading of prophetic words, keeping alive the memory of Jerusalem in prayers and by collections for the city's survivors, and urging support for the Babylonian rulers. This reconstruction overlooks the fact that Baruch was taken to Egypt along with Jeremiah (Jer 43:5-7). The author or compiler, writing five hundred years after the fall of Jerusalem and the deportation, seeks to rouse in his contemporaries a sense of their historic roots at a time when Hebrew life is quieter and easier and in some danger of absorption by other religious and social currents. He wants the people of God of his own time to experience solidarity with their ancestors of exilic times and also to be aware of the sinful tendencies which led to the downfall in the past and which are still lurking.

Like other biblical writings of the time (Daniel, Tobit, Judith, Esther), Baruch uses history only as a framework for its message. Historical anachronisms and mistakes abound, particularly in the introductory verses (1:1-14). This alarms today's reader with a modern scientific notion of historical writing, but the first century B.C. editor would have shrugged off any charge of inaccuracy: "So what? The exile did happen, and my message is true; so why bother about minor details?" In commenting on the book, I will point out inaccuracies and chronological complications, legitimate concerns for today's reader, remembering all the while that the meaning of the book is little affected by these questions.

BY THE WATERS OF BABYLON
1:1-4

1 These are the words of the book which Baruch the son of Neraiah, son of Mahseiah, son of Zedekiah, son of Hasadiah, son of Hilkiah, wrote in Babylon, ²in the fifth year, on the seventh day of the month, at the time when the Chaldeans took Jerusalem and burned it with fire.³And Baruch read the words of this book in the hearing of Jeconiah the son of Jehoiakim, king of Judah, and in the hearing of all the people who came to hear the book, ⁴and in the hearing of the mighty men and the princes, and in the hearing of the elders, and in the hearing of all the people, small and great, all who dwelt in Babylon by the river Sud.

The time of Baruch's activity is "the fifth year, on the seventh day of the month, at the time when the Chaldeans took Jerusalem and burned it with fire" (v.2). This would seem to mean the seventh day of Ab, the fifth month (July-August), which in 582 B.C. would have been the fifth anniversary of the destruction of the Temple (2 Kgs 25:8). Jeconiah (or Jehoiachin) had ruled in Jerusalem for only three months in 597 B.C. before he was captured and taken to Babylon by Nebuchadnezzar, there to be kept under house arrest (2 Kgs 24:8-15). He is presented here as the focus of hope for the exiles dwelling by the river Sud, presumably one of the Babylonian canals (v.4), in the manner that Ezekiel the prophet gave hope to the community gathered by the canal Chebar (Ezek 1:1). Another dating possibility is to calculate the "fifth year" from the deportation of Jeconiah (which would make the date 592 B.C.), because the Jerusalem Temple still seems to be standing (vv.10-14). On the other hand, incense was offered in the ruined Temple area after its destruction (Jer 41:5), and the author's purpose is better served if the scene is set after the total destruction.

MISSION TO JERUSALEM
1:5-14

⁵Then they wept, and fasted, and prayed before the Lord; ⁶and they collected money, each giving what he could; ⁷and they sent it to Jerusalem to Jehoiakim the high priest, the son of Hilkiah, son of Shallum, and to the priests, and to all the people who were present with him in Jerusalem. ⁸At the same time, on the tenth day of Sivan, Baruch took the vessels of the house of the Lord, which had been carried away from the temple, to return them to the land of Judah—the silver vessels which Zedekiah the son of Josiah, king of Judah, had made, ⁹after Nebuchadnezzar king of Babylon had

carried away from Jerusalem Jeconiah and the princes and the prisoners and the mighty men and the people of the land, and brought them to Babylon. [10]And they said: "Herewith we send you money; so buy with the money burnt offerings and sin offerings and incense, and prepare a cereal offering, and offer them upon the altar of the Lord our God; [11]and pray for the life of Nebuchadnezzar king of Babylon, and for the life of Belshazzar his son, that their days on earth may be like the days of heaven. [12]And the Lord will give us strength, and he will give light to our eyes, and we shall live under the protection of Nebuchadnezzar king of Babylon, and under the protection of Belshazzar his son, and we shall serve them many days and find favor in their sight. [13]And pray for us to the Lord our God, for we have sinned against the Lord our God, and to this day the anger of the Lord and his wrath have not turned away from us. [14]And you shall read this book which we are sending you, to make your confession in the house of the Lord on the days of the feasts and at appointed seasons.

Even in the midst of their own suffering the exiles were thinking of the plight of Jerusalem (vv.5-7). The practice arose of assigning fixed days for prayer and fasting by the exiles to make amends for the sin which led to punishment. This continued into post-exilic times (Zech 7:1-5; Ezra 8:21; Neh 1:4; 9:1) to give the descendants of the exiles a sense of solidarity with the past suffering. The concern for Jerusalem is highlighted by a collection taken up among the dispossessed exiles (v.6). Baruch carries this as well as some of the vessels from the Temple back to Jerusalem (v.8). All of this is very unlikely—the early unmolested return to Jerusalem, the mention of a restoration of silver vessels nowhere else recorded, the naming of a high priest (v.7) not otherwise known—but it serves the author's purpose in describing the indomitable fidelity of the exiles. The incidental details are just scenery.

The message sent to Jerusalem asks for prayers for the Babylonian rulers and for the exiles themselves (vv.11-13). This attitude toward exile is a reflection of Jeremiah's instructions: "Seek the welfare of the city where I have sent you into exile, and pray to the Lord on its behalf, for in its welfare you will find your welfare" (Jer 29:7). By picturing Nebuchadnezzar and Belshazzar as father and son (as also Dan 5:2), the tradition managed to compress the whole Exile into one phrase. Historically Nebuchadnezzar was the agent of the destruction and deportation of 587 B.C., while Belshazzar was the son and co-regent of Nabonidus, the last Chaldean ruler of Babylon, dethroned by Cyrus the Persian who put an end to the Exile in 538 B.C.

THE LORD KEPT HIS WORD
1:15 - 2:10

[15]"And you shall say: 'Righteousness belongs to the Lord our God, but confusion of face, as at this day, to us, to the men of Judah, to the inhabitants of Jerusalem, [16]and to our kings and our princes and our priests and our prophets and our fathers, [17]because we have sinned before the Lord, [18]and have disobeyed him, and have not heeded the voice of the Lord our God, to walk in the statutes of the Lord which he set before us. [19]From the day when the Lord brought our fathers out of the land of Egypt until today, we have been disobedient to the Lord our God, and we have been negligent, in not heeding his voice. [20]So to this day there have clung to us the calamities and the curse which the Lord declared through Moses his servant at the time when he brought our fathers out of the land of Egypt to give to us a land flowing with milk and honey. [21]We did not heed the voice of the Lord our God in all the words of the prophets whom he sent to us, but we each followed the intent of his own wicked heart by serving other gods and doing what is evil in the sight of the Lord our God.

2 "'So the Lord confirmed his word, which he spoke against us, and against our judges who judged Israel, and against our kings and against our princes and against the men of Israel and Judah. ²Under the whole heaven there has not been done the like of what he has done in Jerusalem, in accordance with what is written in the law of Moses, ³that we should eat, one the flesh of his son and another the flesh of his daughter. ⁴And he gave them into subjection to all the kingdoms around us, to be a reproach and a desolation among all the surrounding peoples, where the Lord has scattered them. ⁵They were brought low and not raised up, because we sinned against the Lord our God, in not heeding his voice.

⁶"'Righteousness belongs to the Lord our God, but confusion of face to us and our fathers, as at this day. ⁷All those calamities with which the Lord threatened us have come upon us. ⁸Yet we have not entreated the favor of the Lord by turning away, each of us, from the thoughts of his wicked heart. ⁹And the Lord has kept the calamities ready, and the Lord has brought them upon us, for the Lord is righteous in all his works which he has commanded us to do. ¹⁰Yet we have not obeyed his voice, to walk in the statutes of the Lord which he set before us.

The long prayer beginning in verse 15 will continue up to 3:8. The exiles explain the reasons for their suffering and admit that they have been justly punished. The prayer is meant for a synagogue service and is similar to other post-exilic formulations, especially the prayer in Daniel 9:4-19 (see also Ezra 9:6-15 Neh 1:5-11; 9:6-37). This first section is a confession before the prayer proper begins (2:11). The opening words are a keynote and refrain: "Righteousness belongs to the Lord our God, but confusion of face to us" (1:15; 2:6).

The disobedience of Israel is traced all the way back to the desert (1:19). There are overtones of the Book of

Deuteronomy in the recital of past deeds of the Lord, and
the curse mentioned is recorded in that book (1:20; Deut
28:15-16; see also Lev 26:14-15). Deuteronomy is also
similar to Baruch as a book composed at a time much later
than the events it records to make the later generation aware
of its heritage.

Because of Israel's disregard for the word of the Lord
which came to her through so many privileged channels,
she has been punished in unheard of ways, above all by
the cannibalism to which the Exile reduced her people
(2:2-3; Jer 19:9; Lam 2:20). The emphasis is on God's
fidelity and his fulfillment of promises, even the curses
which "clung to us" (1:20). Even though the people knew
this, they tried to shake off the curse, seeking protection
from other gods. They admit that they did not call on him,
so his punishment is justified (2:8-9).

FOR THY OWN SAKE DELIVER US
2:11-26

[11]"'And now, O Lord God of Israel, who didst bring
thy people out of the land of Egypt with a mighty hand
and with signs and wonders and with great power and
outstretched arm, and hast made thee a name, as at this
day, [12]we have sinned, we have been ungodly, we have
done wrong, O Lord our God, against all thy ordinances.
[13]Let thy anger turn away from us, for we are left, few in
number, among the nations where thou hast scattered us.
[14]Hear, O Lord, our prayer and our supplication, and
for thy own sake deliver us, and grant us favor in the
sight of those who have carried us into exile; [15]that all the
earth may know that thou art the Lord our God, for
Israel and his descendants are called by thy name.
[16]O Lord, look down from thy holy habitation, and
consider us. Incline thy ear, O Lord, and hear; [17]open
thy eyes, O Lord, and see; for the dead who are in Hades,
whose spirit has been taken from their bodies, will not

ascribe glory or justice to the Lord, [18]but the person that is greatly distressed, that goes about bent over and feeble, and the eyes that are failing, and the person that hungers, will ascribe to thee glory and righteousness, O Lord. [19]For it is not because of any righteous deeds of our fathers or our kings that we bring before thee our prayer for mercy, O Lord our God. [20]For thou hast sent thy anger and thy wrath upon us, as thou didst declare by thy servants the prophets, saying: [21]"Thus says the Lord: Bend your shoulders and serve the king of Babylon, and you will remain in the land which I gave to your fathers. [22]But if you will not obey the voice of the Lord and will not serve the king of Babylon, [23]I will make to cease from the cities of Judah and from the region about Jerusalem the voice of mirth and the voice of gladness, the voice of the bridegroom and the voice of the bride, and the whole land will be a desolation without inhabitants."

[24]"But we did not obey thy voice, to serve the king of Babylon; and thou hast confirmed thy words, which thou didst speak by thy servants the prophets, that the bones of our kings and the bones of our fathers would be brought out of their graves; [25]and behold, they have been cast out to the heat of day and the frost of night. They perished in great misery, by famine and sword and pestilence. [26]And the house which is called by thy name thou hast made as it is today, because of the wickedness of the house of Israel and the house of Judah.

The exiles begin their prayer by addressing Yahweh with a title which identifies him in terms of the great saving acts of the past (v.11). Again the phraseology has the ring of Deuteronomy (4:34; 6:21-22). Now the people repeat for the Lord the self-recriminations they had rehearsed for their compatriots (v.13; 1:17-21). They base their request for relief on two arguments: it is in God's best interests to bless his people, for then all the world will know his glory (v.15); if his people are killed they will not be able to praise him (v.17). The appeal to enlightened self-interest we have noted in Joel 2:17 (see Is 38:18-20). The warning about killing one's worshipers appears also in the Psalms (Pss 6:5; 88:10). A person who dies goes to "Hades" (Greek v.17) or "Sheol" (Hebrew), the "land of the shadows" which is the final goal of all. We do not detect the resurrection faith that emerged in other biblical writings of this era (Dan 12:2; 2 Macc 7:9-14). This omission is another reason some scholars argue for an early date for Baruch.

The failure to listen to the prophets (1:21) is interpreted above all as ignoring Jeremiah's instruction to cooperate with the Babylonian invaders and make the best of life in exile (Jer 27:12-13). The desecration of ancestral graves (vv.24-25) is nowhere else attested, though such profana-tions were known in the Ancient Near East as an expression of utter contempt for a subjugated people. This is probably the imagined fulfillment of Jeremiah 8:1-2. Careful burial was important, because the shadow-part of an individual in Sheol was thought to experience what happened to the body. There was great fear of being left unburied, the prey of wild animals (Jer 16:4; Ezek 29:5).

THE PRAYER OF THE DEAD
2:27 - 3:8

> [27]"'Yet thou hast dealt with us, O Lord our God, in all thy kindness and in all thy great compassion, [28]as thou didst speak by thy servant Moses on the day when thou didst command him to write thy law in the presence of the people of Israel, saying, [29]"If you will not obey my voice, this very great multitude will surely turn into a small number among the nations, where I will scatter them. [30]For I know that they will not obey me, for they are a stiff-necked people. But in the land of their exile they will come to themselves, [31]and they will know that I am the Lord their God. I will give them a heart that

obeys and ears that hear; [32]and they will praise me in
the land of their exile, and will remember my name, [33]and
will turn from their stubbornness and their wicked deeds;
for they will remember the ways of their fathers, who
sinned before the Lord. [34]I will bring them again into
the land which I swore to give to their fathers, to
Abraham and to Isaac and to Jacob, and they will rule
over it; and I will increase them, and they will not be
diminished. [35]I will make an everlasting covenant with
them to be their God and they shall be my people; and
I will never again remove my people Israel from the land
which I have given them."

3 "'O Lord Almighty, God of Israel, the soul in anguish
and the wearied spirit cry out to thee. [2]Hear, O Lord,
and have mercy, for we have sinned before thee. [3]For
thou art enthroned for ever, and we are perishing for ever.
[4]O Lord Almighty, God of Israel, hear now the prayer
of the dead of Israel and of the sons of those who sinned
before thee, who did not heed the voice of the Lord their
God, so that calamities have clung to us. [5]Remember
not the iniquities of our fathers, but in this crisis remember thy power and thy name. [6]For thou art the Lord
our God, and thee, O Lord, will we praise. [7]For thou hast
put the fear of thee in our hearts in order that we should
call upon thy name; and we will praise thee in our exile,
for we have put away from our hearts all the iniquity of
our fathers who sinned before thee.[8]Behold, we are today
in our exile where thou hast scattered us, to be re-
proached and cursed and punished for all the iniquities
of our fathers who forsook the Lord our God.'"

The exiles' prayer turns to a remembrance of the goodness
of the Lord to his people in giving them the Law (2:27-28).
The Mosaic Law is not a curse or a burden, but a great
gift. The promise of exile and return is a mixture of texts
from Deuteronomy (30:1-10; 31:24-27). Even the Exile is

not seen as pure punishment, but as an opportunity for self-knowledge and conversion (2:30-31). They will be able henceforward to hear the word of God and do it. The promise of an everlasting covenant recalls Jeremiah's prophecy of a new covenant (Jer 31:31-34).

The final section of the prayer is more impassioned: "Hear, O Lord, and have mercy"! (3:2). The exiles speak of themselves as already "dead" because of the depth of their loss and misery (3:4; see Isa 59:10; Lam 3:6). Ezekiel had compared the whole nation of Israel exiled in Babylon to a field of dry bones waiting for restoration (Ezek 37:1-14). The suffering of Jerusalem was attributed to the sins of preceding generations as well as of the current one. The exiles ask that Yahweh start over in his relationship with his people, forgetting their former sins and "remembering" his own power and name (3:5). "Remembering" in this sense is not simply calling to mind but making the reality an active force in practice. The people "forgot" God's sovereignty when they sinned and "remembered" it when they remained true to him (Ps 78:11,35). Now "in this crisis" (3:5) they do not want to be forgotten.

IN PRAISE OF DIVINE WISDOM
3:9-23

> [9] Hear the commandments of life, O Israel;
>   give ear, and learn wisdom!
> [10] Why is it, O Israel, why is it that you are
>   in the land of your enemies,
>   that you are growing old in a foreign country,
>   that you are defiled with the dead,
> [11] that you are counted among those in Hades?
> [12] You have forsaken the fountain of wisdom.
> [13] If you had walked in the way of God,
>   you would be dwelling in peace for ever.

¹⁴Learn where there is wisdom,
   where there is strength,
   where there is understanding,
that you may at the same time discern
   where there is length of days, and life,
   where there is light for the eyes, and peace.

¹⁵Who has found her place?
   And who has entered her storehouses?
¹⁶Where are the princes of the nations,
   and those who rule over the beasts on the earth;
¹⁷those who have sport with the birds of the air,
   and who hoard up silver and gold,
in which men trust,
   and there is no end to their getting;
¹⁸those who scheme to get silver, and are anxious,
   whose labors are beyond measure?
¹⁹They have vanished and gone down to Hades,
   and others have arisen in their place.

²⁰Young men have seen the light of day,
   and have dwelt upon the earth;
but they have not learned the way to knowledge,
   nor understood her paths,
   nor laid hold of her.
²¹Their sons have strayed far from her way.
²²She has not been heard of in Canaan,
   nor seen in Teman;
²³the sons of Hagar, who seek for understanding on
   the earth,
   the merchants of Merran and Teman,
   the story-tellers and the seekers for understanding,
have not learned the way to wisdom,
   nor given thought to her paths.

The change from verse 8 to verse 9 is abrupt: prose to poetry, confession and petition to praise of divine wisdom.

There is also suddenly contact with the thought and expressions of the wisdom literature, particularly Proverbs, Job and Sirach. Sin in this section is closer to stupidity than malice.

In the opening lines Israel is addressed as if she were still in exile (vv.10-11), but this is only a literary device to connect this poem with the setting intended by the author. Once mentioned the point is forgotten for the rest of the poem (which ends at 4:4). Israel's deportation is due to her sinfulness, a sinfulness defined here as willful ignorance of divine wisdom (v.12). The Babylonians, who have not been given this wisdom, the source of life, are described as "dead"; they defile the Israelites as would contact with a corpse (v.10; Num 19:11). The fact that just a few verses earlier (v.4) the Israelites themselves were described as "dead" is another indication of the multiple sources of the material in Baruch. Existence without wisdom is no better than the semi-existence of Hades. The fountain of wisdom is Yahweh himself; the ultimate gift of his wisdom, described beautifully in verse 14, is peace, the same kind of peace which according to Paul "passes all understanding" (Phil 4:7).

The hymn to wisdom proper begins with verse 15, where wisdom is personified as in other late Old Testament writings (Prov 1:20; 8; Sir 24:1; Wis 7:7-30; 10:1). The theme is repeated over and over with the help of various images: wisdom is beyond human reach or control (Job 28:1-24). The reference to a cache or storehouse of wisdom touches a characteristic theme in the literature (v.15; Job 28:1,12). The rich and mighty of the world come and go, but wisdom remains. The merchants, the hunters, the philosophers seek for true wisdom but in vain (vv.17-18, 23). Even the places associated with wisdom do not have the authentic article: Canaan (Ezek 28:3-5), Teman (the homeland of Eliphaz, one of Job's "wise" friends), Merran (possibly a mistake for Midian: NAB, JB), and the Ishmaelite territory in Northwest Arabia (vv.23-24; Gen 25:18). All of this is a grand crescendo making the point that even the whole of creation cannot possess or contain wisdom unless God gives it.

GOD AND THE UNIVERSE
3:24 - 4:4

24O Israel, how great is the house of God!
  And how vast the territory that he possesses!
25It is great and has no bounds;
  it is high and immeasurable.
26The giants were born there, who were famous of old,
  great in stature, expert in war.
27God did not choose them,
  nor give them the way to knowledge;
28so they perished because they had no wisdom,
  they perished through their folly.
29Who has gone up into heaven, and taken her,
  and brought her down from the clouds?
30Who has gone over the sea, and found her,
  and will buy her for pure gold?
31No one knows the way to her,
  or is concerned about the path to her.
32But he who knows all things knows her,
  he found her by his understanding.
He who prepared the earth for all time
  filled it with four-footed creatures;
33he who sends forth the light, and it goes,
  called it, and it obeyed him in fear;
34the stars shone in their watches, and were glad;
  he called them, and they said, "Here we are!"
  They shone with gladness for him who made them.
35This is our God;
  no other can be compared to him!
36He found the whole way to knowledge,
  and gave her to Jacob his servant
  and to Israel whom he loved,

37Afterward she appeared upon earth
and lived among men.

4 She is the book of the commandments of God,
and the law that endures for ever.
All who hold her fast will live,
and those who forsake her will die.
2Turn, O Jacob, and take her;
walk toward the shining of her light.
3Do not give your glory to another,
or your advantages to an alien people.
4Happy we are, O Israel,
for we know what is pleasing to God.

"How great is the house of God!" (3:24). In the psalms this familiar phrase would refer to the Jerusalem Temple (Pss 23:6; 27:4; 42:4; 84:4; 122:1). In this poem it means the whole universe. There does not appear in this usage to be any of the anti-Temple polemic (or rather reaction against the super-idealization of the Temple) found in Jeremiah (Jer 7:4) and some post-exilic traditions (Isa 66:1). But by this time a more transcendent notion of God is to the fore. He fills the universe (3:32-34). Later, Stephen voices an extreme Hellenistic bias against the Temple, using arguments from God's lordship over creation (Acts 7:48-50).

The mention of giants (3:26) harks back to Genesis folklore (Gen 6:4; see Wis 14:6). Great as they were, the giants could not find wisdom because they were not chosen, and without wisdom they perished (3:27-28). The rhetorical questions "Who has gone up? . . . . Who has gone over?" were used earlier in the biblical tradition to underscore the inaccessibility of the divine law (Deut 30:12-13) and wisdom (Job 28:12-14). St. Paul applied the theme to bring Christ, the law, justice, and the word of God into a new synthesis (Rom 10:4-8). The answer to the question here will be spelled out in the subsequent verses: only God can find and control wisdom.

God is the master of creation; it holds no mysteries for him. Sunrise and sunset are acts of obedience to him by the sun (3:33). The stars are like sentries on the watch: their twinkling is a response of happiness for the presence of the master (3:24). God "found" wisdom and gave her as a gift to his chosen people. "She appeared upon earth and lived among men" (3:37). The Old Latin translation of the second or third century A.D. changed the pronoun to "He" to make this verse a prediction of the Incarnation. In a surprising change of thought, wisdom, until now personified as an elusive and superior being, is equated with the "book of the commandments of God" (4:1). This is a clear sign that 4:1-4 belongs with 3:9-14, also dealing with "commandments," and has been separated by the later wisdom poem in 3:15-37. The Torah has been entrusted to Israel; if it is not followed, the Lord may take it away and give it to another people (4:3). Thus Israel would no longer have happiness, which consists in knowing what pleases the Lord (4:4). The influence of the Book of Deuteronomy, noted frequently, is evident here, too, in the connection of the divine law and wisdom (Deut 4:5-8; 30:11-18). It should be mentioned that 3:34 of the Revised Standard Version is two verses in the Greek and many English translations (for example, JB, NAB).

JERUSALEM AND HER CHILDREN
4:5-29

> 5Take courage, my people,
>   O memorial of Israel!
> 6It was not for destruction
>   that you were sold to the nations,
> but you were handed over to your enemies
>   because you angered God.
> 7For you provoked him who made you,
>   by sacrificing to demons and not to God.

⁸You forgot the everlasting God, who brought you up,
   and you grieved Jerusalem, who reared vou
⁹For sne saw the wrath that came upon you from God,
   and she said:
"Hearken, you neighbors of Zion,
   God hás brought great sorrow upon me;
¹⁰for I have seen the captivity of my sons and daughters,
   which the Everlasting brought upon them.
¹¹With joy I nurtured them,
   but I sent them away with weeping and sorrow.
¹²Let no one rejoice over me, a widow
   and bereaved of many;
I was left desolate because of the sins of my children,
   because they turned away from the law of God.
¹³They had no regard for his statutes;
   they did not walk in the ways of God's commandments,
   nor tread the paths of discipline in his righteousness.
¹⁴Let the neighbors of Zion come;
   remember the capture of my sons and daughters,
   which the Everlasting brought upon them.
¹⁵For he brought against them a nation from afar,
   a shameless nation, of a strange language,
who had no respect for an old man,
   and had no pity for a child.
¹⁶They led away the widow's beloved sons,
   and bereaved the lonely woman of her daughters.

¹⁷"But I, how can I help you?
¹⁸For he who brought these calamities upon you
   will deliver you from the hand of your enemies.
¹⁹Go, my children, go;
   for I have been left desolate.
²⁰I have taken off the robe of peace
   and put on the sackcloth of my supplication;
   I will cry to the Everlasting all my days.

²¹"Take courage, my children, cry to God,
   and he will deliver you from the power and hand
      of the enemy.

²²For I have put my hope in the Everlasting to save you,
    and joy has come to me from the Holy One,
because of the mercy which soon will come to you
    from your everlasting Savior.
²³For I sent you out with sorrow and weeping,
    but God will give you back to me with joy and
        gladness for ever.
²⁴For as the neighbors of Zion have now seen your
    capture,
    so they soon will see your salvation by God,
which will come to you with great glory
    and with the splendor of the Everlasting.
²⁵My children, endure with patience
    the wrath that has come upon you from God.
Your enemy has overtaken you,
    but you will soon see their destruction
    and will tread upon their necks.
²⁶My tender sons have traveled rough roads;
    they were taken away like a flock carried off
        by the enemy.

²⁷"Take courage, my children, and cry to God,
    for you will be remembered by him who brought
        this upon you.
²⁸For just as you purposed to go astray from God,
    return with tenfold zeal to seek him.
²⁹For he who brought these calamities upon you
    will bring you everlasting joy with your salvation."

A new poem (4:5 - 5:9) addresses the exiles themselves, exhorting them to courage and perseverance in their
place of foreign bondage. Even in exile, they are still
Yahweh's people called by the ancient name, Israel, and are
a living memorial of Jerusalem and the Temple, and of
God's election (v.5). Yahweh is described as the "everlasting God" (vv.8,10) in contrast to the "demons" (idols)
who were always drawing Israel away. The transcendence
and universal lordship of Yahweh was a lesson learned and

deepened in the Exile. The people can take courage because it was not for annihilation that they were given up to their enemies, but for a punishment for sin that will be followed by mercy and salvation (vv.21-22). Now it is Jerusalem instead of wisdom who is personified: Jerusalem the mother who nurtured her children and now mourns because of their distress. The influence of the exilic prophet known as Second Isaiah (Isa 40 - 55) is apparent in the description of Jerusalem and her children suffering in exile (see Isa 49:21; 51:18) and in the message of consolation that breaks through from the Lord (see Isa 40:1-2).

The first four and a half verses (4:5-9a) serve as an introduction for the words of Mother Jerusalem to her exiled children. Direct appeals separate the poem into stanzas: "hearken!" (v.9), "come!" (v.14), "take courage!" (vv.21,27). Mother Jerusalem speaks of the plight that has befallen her children, but without the bitterness and hopelessness of Lamentations. The children are punished because they have sinned: God has acted justly (v.12). But the God who punished will also restore. Jerusalem prays for her children and urges courage and patience until the time comes. It is a prayer of firm hope: "I have put my hope in the Everlasting to save you" (v.21). When the restoration comes, Jerusalem's neighbors (here described as friendly: vv.14,24) will witness Yahweh's power and glory. A post-exilic psalm captures the exhilaration of the Israelites and the awe of the nations at the time of the return from exile:

"When the Lord restored the fortunes of Zion,
  we were like those who dream.
Then our mouth was filled with laughter,
  and our tongue with shouts of joy;
then they said among the nations,
  'The Lord has done great things for them.'
The Lord has done great things for us; we are glad."
                                                    (Ps 126:1-3)

STAND UPON THE HEIGHT
4:30 - 5:9

30Take courage, O Jerusalem,
for he who named you will comfort you.
31Wretched will be those who afflicted you
and rejoiced at your fall.
32Wretched will be the cities which your children
served as slaves;
wretched will be the city which received your sons.
33For just as she rejoiced at your fall and was glad
for your ruin,
so she will be grieved at her own desolation.
34And I will take away her pride in her great population,
and her insolence will be turned to grief.
35For fire will come upon her from the Everlasting
for many days,
and for a long time she will be inhabited by demons.

36Look toward the east, O Jerusalem,
and see the joy that is coming to you from God!
37Behold, your sons are coming, whom you sent away;
they are coming, gathered from east and west,
at the word of the Holy One,
rejoicing in the glory of God.

5   Take off the garment of your sorrow and affliction,
O Jerusalem,
and put on for ever the beauty of the glory of God.
2Put on the robe of the righteousness from God;
put on your head the diadem of the glory of the
Everlasting.
3For God will show your splendor everywhere
under heaven.
4For your name will for ever be called by God,
"Peace of righteousness and glory of godliness."

5Arise, O Jerusalem, stand upon the height
and look toward the east,

and see your children gathered from west and east,
   at the word of the Holy One,
   rejoicing that God has remembered them.
⁶For they went forth from you on foot,
   led away by their enemies;
but God will bring them back to you,
   carried in glory, as on a royal throne.
⁷For God has ordered that every high
   mountain and the everlasting
   hills be made low
   and the valleys filled up, to make level ground,
   so that Israel may walk safely in the glory of God.
⁸The woods and every fragrant tree
   have shaded Israel at God's command.
⁹For God will lead Israel with joy,
   in the light of his glory,
   with the mercy and righteousness that come from him.

Jerusalem has been encouraging her children to fortitude
and patience; now she becomes the object of encouragement herself: "Take courage, O Jerusalem" (4:30). The
return from exile is much closer than in the preceding section.
The city is comforted with the knowledge that she is
Yahweh's own city. She is known by his name and can
trust him to share with her his own qualities of peace and
righteousness, even his own glory (5:4). The terminology
is familiar from earlier prophets: a reversal is sure to come
to the proud oppressors of Israel (4:31-35). Babylon will be
inhabited by demons, a sign that she has become a desolate
waste (see Isa 13:21-22).

Jerusalem is urged to rise from her bed of sorrow and
look to the east: see the joy that is coming, take off the
garment of sorrow, put on the robe of righteousness and the
diadem (4:36 - 5:2). But the author of Baruch is only using
the setting of the Exile as imagery to carry a message for
his contemporaries. The restoration he is envisioning is the
final messianic age in which the children will be gathered

not only from the east (Babylon) but from east and west (everywhere: 4:37; 5:5). Baruch's contemporary audience and even his readers today are included in this vision. We have gone astray and been taken into exile. God will bring us all back to him and together we will march to the new Jerusalem. The imagery of Second Isaiah is easily recognizable: hills lowered, valleys filled (Isa 40:3-4). Baruch adds that the trees will bend to shade the path of the returnees (5:8). God's people will be borne in like royalty (5:6).

THE LETTER OF JEREMIAH
6:1-7

6 A copy of a letter which Jeremiah sent to those who were to be taken to Babylon as captives by the king of the Babylonians, to give them the message which God had commanded him.

²Because of the sins which you have committed before God, you will be taken to Babylon as captives by Nebuchadnezzar, king of the Babylonians. ³Therefore when you have come to Babylon you will remain there for many years, for a long time, up to seven generations; after that I will bring you away from there in peace. ⁴Now in Babylon you will see gods made of silver and gold and wood, which are carried on men's shoulders and inspire fear in the heathen. ⁵So take care not to become at all like the foreigners or to let fear for these gods possess you, when you see the multitude before and behind them worshiping them. ⁶But say in your heart, "It is thou, O Lord, whom we must worship." ⁷For my angel is with you, and he is watching your lives.

Baruch 6 was originally a free-floating warning against idolatry addressed to Jews living in the Dispersion. Verse 1, attributing it to Jeremiah, is a later addition modeled on the introduction to the prophet's letter to the Hebrews taken to Babylon in 597 B.C. (Jer 29:1). In the Greek Bible this chapter is treated as an independent writing under the title "Letter of Jeremiah" and is separated from the Book of Baruch by Lamentations. In the Latin Vulgate (followed by Catholic Bibles and RSV editions containing the Apocrypha) the Letter forms Chapter Six of Baruch and is followed by Lamentations. The Letter is alluded to in 2 Maccabees 2:1-3 (which was written after 124 B.C.). A scroll fragment (dated to 100 B.C.) containing verses 43-44 in Greek was discovered among the Dead Sea Scrolls in Cave VII at Qumran.

The anonymous author has modified Jeremiah's prophecy of an exile of seventy years (Jer 25:11) to "up to seven generations" (v.3), possibly revealing the date of his writing. If a generation is taken as forty years, as traditional in biblical numerology (Judg 3:11, 30), seven generations from the deportation would bring us to around 300 B.C. In this case, the Letter of Jeremiah could be much older than the other chapters of Baruch, to which it was added later. By connecting contemporary events with the promise of Jeremiah, the author of the Letter, like his colleague in Baruch 5, is keeping the faith of a later generation of Hebrews alive with a reminder of the final restoration due at any moment.

Thoughts on the ridiculousness of idolatry tumble forth with no particular order. The letter's mood fluctuates between subtly ironic to sarcastic. It is held together by a number of refrains repeating the conclusion that the idols are not gods and should not be feared (vv.5,16,23,29, 65,69); and of course they cannot give salvation (vv.49,52). The frequent mention of fear indicates that their foreign neighbors were threatening the Hebrews with dire consequences if they did not pacify the local gods. But the chosen people, whether in exile or dispersion or in Jerusalem, must recall the lordship of Yahweh: "It is thou, O Lord, whom we must worship" (v.6).

LIFELESS IDOLS
6:8-29

⁸Their tongues are smoothed by the craftsman, and they themselves are overlaid with gold and silver; but they are false and cannot speak. ⁹People take gold and make crowns for the heads of their gods, as they would for a girl who loves ornaments; ¹⁰and sometimes the priests secretly take gold and silver from their gods and spend it upon themselves, ¹¹and even give some of it to the harlots in the brothel. They deck their gods out with garments like men—these gods of silver and gold and wood, ¹²which cannot save themselves from rust and corrosion. When they have been dressed in purple robes, ¹³their faces are wiped because of the dust from the temple, which is thick upon them. ¹⁴Like a local ruler the god holds a scepter, though unable to destroy any one who offends it. ¹⁵It has a dagger in its right hand, and has an axe; but it cannot save itself from war and robbers. ¹⁶Therefore they evidently are not gods; so do not fear them.

¹⁷For just as one's dish is useless when it is broken, so are the gods of the heathen, when they have been set up in the temples. Their eyes are full of the dust raised by the feet of those who enter. ¹⁸And just as the gates are shut on every side upon a man who has offended a king, as though he were sentenced to death, so the priests make their temples secure with doors and locks and bars, in order that they may not be plundered by robbers. ¹⁹They light lamps, even more than they light for themselves, though their gods can see none of them. ²⁰They are just like a beam of the temple, but men say their hearts have melted, when worms from the earth devour them and their robes. They do not notice ²¹when their faces have been blackened by the smoke of the temple. ²²Bats, swallows, and birds light on their bodies and heads; and so do cats. ²³From this you will know that they are not gods; so do not fear them.

²⁴As for the gold which they wear for beauty—they will not shine unless some one wipes off the rust; for even when they were being cast, they had no feeling. ²⁵They are bought at any cost, but there is no breath in them. ²⁶Having no feet, they are carried on men's shoulders, revealing to mankind their worthlessness. ²⁷And those who serve them are ashamed because through them these gods are made to stand, lest they fall to the ground. If any one sets one of them upright, it cannot move of itself; and if it is tipped over, it cannot straighten itself; but gifts are placed before them just as before the dead. ²⁸The priests sell the sacrifices that are offered to these gods and use the money; and likewise their wives preserve some with salt, but give none to the poor or helpless. ²⁹Sacrifices to them may be touched by women in menstruation or at childbirth. Since you know by these things that they are not gods, do not fear them.

The ridicule of idols begins with the statement that their expensive exterior is only skin-deep: they are wood overlaid with precious metal (v.8). A practical reason was behind this: they could not be too heavy to carry in procession. The idols are compared to a giddy girl being decked with ornaments (v.9); they have tongues but can't speak (see Ps 115:3-8); they can't use their scepters or daggers (v.15). They are compared to a broken dish (v.17), a wormy temple beam (v.20). They can't move on their own (v.26) and must be locked up for their protection (v.18); bats and cats roost on their heads (v.22). Someone else has to wipe the dust from their faces for them (v.13). The heavy-handed ridicule is similar to (and probably dependent on) passages in Jeremiah (10:1-6) and Isaiah (44:9-20).

A strong sub-theme of the ridicule is the venality of the pagan priests. They are accused of pilfering the precious metal and sharing it with cult prostitutes (vv.10-11); they and their wives keep the altar sacrifices and other provisions for their own use (v.28). Contrasts with standard Hebrew practices are mentioned: they save nothing for the poor (v.28: Deut 14:28-29); they do not observe the laws of ritual purity (v.29: Lev 12:2-3).

WHY CALL THEM GODS?
6:30-52

30For why should they be called gods? Women serve meals for gods of silver and gold and wood; 31and in their temples the priests sit with their clothes rent, their' heads and beards shaved, and their heads uncovered. 32They howl and shout before their gods as some do at a funeral feast for a man who has died. 33The priests take some of the clothing of their gods to clothe their wives and children. 34Whether one does evil to them or good, they will not be able to repay it. They cannot set up a king or depose one. 35Likewise they are not able to give either wealth or money; if one makes a vow to them and does not keep it they will not require it. 36They cannot save a man from death or rescue the weak from the strong. 37They cannot restore sight to a blind man; they cannot rescue a man who is in distress. 38They cannot take pity on a widow or do good to an orphan. 39These things that are made of wood and overlaid with gold and silver are like stones from the mountain, and those who serve them will be put to shame. 40Why then must any one think that they are gods, or call them gods?

Besides, even the Chaldeans themselves dishonor them; 41for when they see a dumb man, who cannot speak, they bring him and pray Bel that the man may speak, as though Bel were able to understand. 42Yet they themselves cannot perceive this and abandon them, for they have no sense. 43And the women, with cords about them, sit along the passageways, burning bran for incense; and when one of them is led off by one of the passers-by and is lain with, she derides the woman next to her, because she was not as attractive as herself and her cord was not broken. ⁴⁴Whatever is done for them is false. Why then must any one think that they are gods, or call them gods?

⁴⁵They are made by carpenters and goldsmiths; they can be nothing but what the craftsmen wish them to be. ⁴⁶The men that make them will certainly not live very long themselves; how then can the things that are made by them be gods? ⁴⁷They have left only lies and reproach for those who come after. ⁴⁸For when war or calamity comes upon them, the priests consult together as to where they can hide themselves and their gods. ⁴⁹How then can one fail to see that these are not gods, for they cannot save themselves from war or calamity? ⁵⁰Since they are made of wood and overlaid with gold and silver, it will afterward be known that they are false. ⁵¹It will be manifest to all the nations and kings that they are not gods but the work of men's hands, and that there is no work of God in them. ⁵²Who then can fail to know that they are not gods?

This section begins on the theme suggested in the closing verses of the preceding: how can the idols be called gods when the service their worshipers render is so vulgar (compared to the worship of Yahweh)? Women serve them meals (v.30), but in proper (Hebrew) religion, only males minister in the Temple. Their priests shave and bare their heads and tear their garments (v.31: contrast Lev 21:5,10). They mourn as if their gods are dead or dying (v.32): this is no doubt a reference to the Babylonian practice of weeping for Tammuz, the god of fertility, in autumn, a rite considered an "abomination" by Israelites (Ezek 8:14-15).

Yahweh has a special place in his heart for the poor, the weak, the widow and the orphan, but an idol cannot come to their aid because of its own helplessness (vv.35-40). The point of verse 41 seems to be that the Chaldeans show just how irreverent they are by bringing a person who cannot speak before their idol, when they know the god cannot even understand people who can speak. The NAB clarifies the verse by translating "deaf mute" instead of "dumb man"; then the foolishness lies in asking their god to speak to one who cannot hear when it cannot speak to those who can hear. "Bel" is the title (corresponding to Hebrew *baal*, master) of the chief Babylonian god, Marduk (Is 46:1). This god is derided at greater length in Daniel 14:3-22.

Babylonian women were required to serve once in their lives as temple prostitutes (vv.43-44). As they sat waiting in the passageway, burning "bran" (an aphrodisiac), each had a cord tied loosely around her. When a woman was chosen for the ritual act, her cord was unfastened. This practice had earlier menaced Israel from contact with Canaanite worship (Hos 4:14). Not only are the idols not gods, "there is no work of God in them" (v.51).

DO NOT FEAR THEM
6:53-73

⁵³For they cannot set up a king over a country or give rain to men. ⁵⁴They cannot judge their own cause or deliver one who is wronged, for they have no power; they are like crows between heaven and earth. ⁵⁵When fire breaks out in a temple of wooden gods overlaid with gold or silver, their priests will flee and escape, but the gods will be burnt in two like beams. ⁵⁶Besides, they can offer no resistance to a king or any enemies. Why then must any one admit or think that they are gods?

⁵⁷Gods made of wood and overlaid with silver and gold are not able to save themselves from thieves and robbers. ⁵⁸Strong men will strip them of their gold and silver and of the robes they wear, and go off with this booty, and they will not be able to help themselves. ⁵⁹So it is better to be a king who shows his courage, or a household utensil that serves its owner's need, than to

be these false gods; better even the door of a house that
protects its contents, than these false gods; better also a
wooden pillar in a palace, than these false gods.
⁶⁰For sun and moon and stars, shining and sent forth
for service, are obedient. ⁶¹So also the lightning, when
it flashes, is widely seen; and the wind likewise blows
in every land. ⁶²When God commands the clouds to go
over the whole world, they carry out his command. ⁶³And
the fire sent from above to consume mountains and
woods does what it is ordered. But these idols are not to
be compared with them in appearance or power. ⁶⁴There-
fore one must not think that they are gods nor call them
gods, for they are not able either to decide a case or to
do good to men. ⁶⁵Since you know then that they are not
gods, do not fear them.
⁶⁶For they can neither curse nor bless kings; ⁶⁷they
cannot show signs in the heavens and among the nations,
or shine like the sun or give light like the moon. ⁶⁸The
wild beasts are better than they are, for they can flee to
cover and help themselves. ⁶⁹So we have no evidence
whatever that they are gods; therefore do not fear them.
⁷⁰Like a scarecrow in a cucumber bed, that guards
nothing, so are their gods of wood, overlaid with gold
and silver. ⁷¹In the same way, their gods of wood, overlaid with gold and silver, are like a thorn bush in a garden,
on which every bird sits; or like a dead body cast out in
the darkness. ⁷²By the purple and linen that rot upon
them you will know that they are not gods; and they
will finally themselves be consumed, and be a reproach
in the land. ⁷³Better therefore is a just man who has no
idols, for he will be far from reproach.

In this closing section the author strains for extreme
comparisons that will remove any lingering doubt about the
idiocy of idol-worship: idols are like crows hanging between
heaven and earth (v.54), or like the scarecrow that drives
them away (v.70); a household utensil is of more use, or a
door or pillar (v.59). An idol is like a thorn bush where

birds perch or, finally, like a corpse (v.71). The images pile up and fall over one another.

By the time the "letter" ends, the redundant argumentation has long since become tedious. As in the case of the diatribe in Isaiah 44:9-20, one wonders whether the author is conversing with a real audience. Were his Israelite readers really in danger of falling for such a crass belief in the power of wooden figurines? Probably not. Probably the idols' devotees would not have owned up to such religion. They courted and feared the power that supposedly lay behind these talismans. It was the belief or suspicion of that power which enslaved them.

The authors of these sarcastic attacks were correct, however, in directing their blows against the idols themselves rather than at some subtle interpretation their theologians might have produced. People are more willing to hold on to things they can see but not understand than things they can understand but not see. We need to remember this ourselves, even though we realize more than the ancients that an "idol" may be visible or invisible and that it takes no special training to create one. Thus the parting word has significance far beyond its ancient context: "Better is a just man who has no idols" (v.73).

Bibliography

J. C. Dancy, *The Shorter Books of the Apocrypha* (Cambridge Bible Commentary). New York and Cambridge: Cambridge University Press, 1972.

C. Moore, "Toward the Dating of the Book of Baruch," *CBQ* 36 (3, 1974), 312-320.

B. Reicke, *The New Testament Era: The World of the Bible From 500 B.C. to A.D. 100*. Philadelphia: Fortress, 1968.

C. Stuhlmueller, *The Books of Jeremiah and Baruch* (Old Testament Reading Guide, 17). Collegeville: Liturgical Press, 1971. Pages 98-112.

220

Related Reading

P. R. Ackroyd, *Exile and Restoration: A Study of Hebrew Thought of the Sixth Century B.C.* (Old Testament Library), Philadelphia: Westminster Press, 1968.
Heavily referenced work interpreting the scholarly debate on the Exile and its immediate aftermath.

B. W. Anderson, *Understanding the Old Testament*, Englewood-Cliffs, N.J. and Hemel Hempstead: Prentice-Hall, second edition, 1966.
Respected introduction often used in Old Testament survey courses. Situates each of the prophets and books studied here in the political, social and religious context.

John Bright, *A History of Israel*, Philadelphia: Westminster Press; London: SCM Press Ltd., second edition, 1972.
A readable history that has become a standard source. The book has helpful chronological charts and maps.

D. R. Hillers, *Lamentations*, Garden City, N.Y.: Doubleday, 1972.
Volume 7A of the Anchor Bible, it follows the series format with a new translation of the text followed by technical notes and a more general commentary.

E. H. Maly, *Prophets of Salvation*, New York: Herder and Herder, 1967.
Chapter Ten of this popular presentation treats most of the prophets studied in this commentary.

B. Reicke, *The New Testament Era: The World of the Bible From 500 B.C. to A.D. 100*, Philadelphia: Fortress Press, 1968.
Very helpful for its light on the political developments affecting post-exilic Judaism.

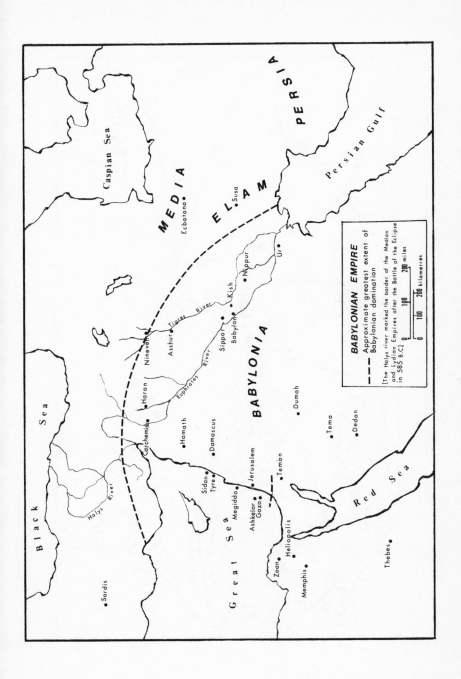

Caspian Sea

MEDIA

PERSIA

ELAM

Persian Gulf

Ecbatana•

•Susa

Black Sea

Nineveh•

Asshur•

Tigris River

•Ur

•Nippur

Kish•

•Babylon

Sippar•

Euphrates River

BABYLONIA

•Haran

•Dumah

Carchemish•

•Hamath

•Damascus

•Tema

•Dedan

Sidon•
Tyre•

Jerusalem•
Megiddo•

•Teman

Ashkelon•
Gaza•

Great Sea

Heliopolis•

Red Sea

Zoan•

•Memphis

•Thebes

Halys River

•Sardis

BABYLONIAN EMPIRE
Approximate greatest extent of
Babylonian domination

[The Halys river marked the border of the Median
and Lydian Empires after the Battle of the Eclipse
in 585 B.C.]

0   100   200 miles
0   100   200 kilometres

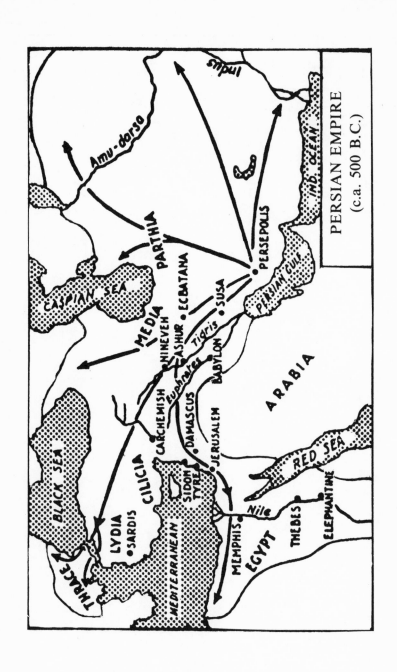

PERSIAN EMPIRE
(c.a. 500 B.C.)

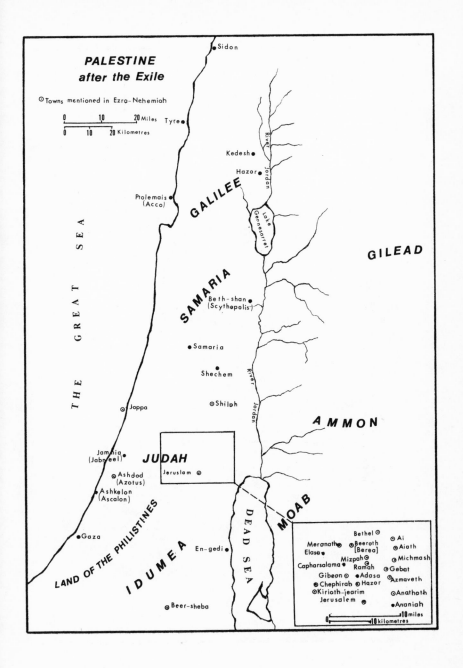

PALESTINE
after the Exile

⊙ Towns mentioned in Ezra-Nehemiah

0   10   20 Miles
0   10   20 Kilometres

Sidon

Tyre

Kedesh

Hazor

Ptolemais
(Acco)

GALILEE

River Jordan

Lake
Gennesarret

GILEAD

T H E   G R E A T   S E A

SAMARIA

Beth-shan
(Scythopolis)

Samaria

Shechem

⊙ Shiloh

River Jordan

AMMON

Joppa

Jamnia
(Jabneel)

JUDAH

Jeruslam ⊙

⊙ Ashdod
(Azotus)

Ashkelon
(Ascalon)

Gaza

L A N D   O F   T H E   P H I L I S T I N E S

IDUMEA

En-gedi

DEAD SEA

MOAB

⊙ Beer-sheba

Bethel ⊙

Meronath ⊙   ⊙ Beeroth   ⊙ Ai
Elasa ●   [Berea]   ⊙ Aiath

Capharsalama ●   Mizpah ⊙   ⊙ Michmash
                    Ramah ⊙   ⊙ Gebat
        Gibeon ⊙   ● Adasa
                                    ⊙ Azmaveth
    ⊙ Chephirah ⊙ Hazor
    ⊙ Kirioth-jearim   ⊙ Anathoth
        Jerusalem ⊙   ● Ananiah

0   10 miles
0   10 kilometres

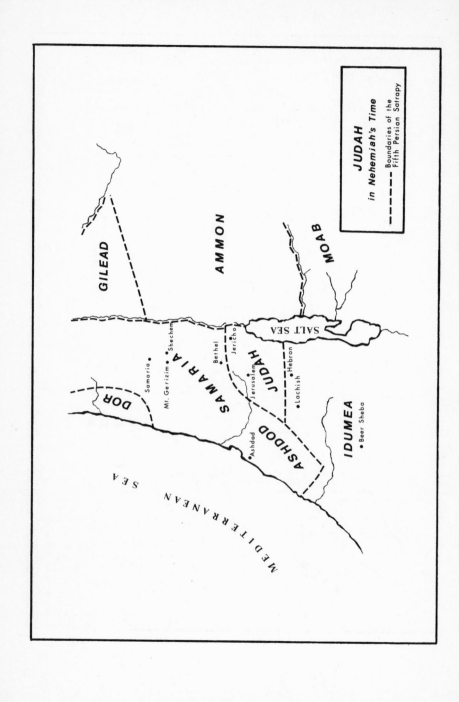

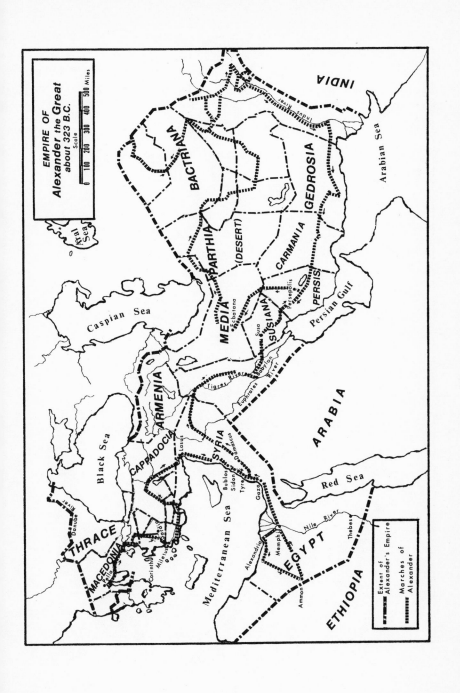